Why School Doesn't Work for Every Child is the clarion call that our education system needs if we are to finally overcome the consequences of disadvantage and inequality that too many children and young people face.

As we have come to expect, Matt Bromley offers insightful and practical advice for schools and educators striving to make a difference for their students from disadvantaged backgrounds.

His ability to distill complex educational concepts into actionable strategies makes his writing a valuable resource for teachers and school leaders at all levels. This is why he is one of SecEd's most prolific and popular authors.

His ideas are grounded in real-world classroom experience, making them both relevant to the challenges schools are facing today and easily adaptable and actionable for your school's context.

Matt Bromley has become one of the most relevant, useful and inspiring voices in education – and this book is no exception.

– Pete Henshaw, *Editor for* SecEd *and* Headteacher Update *magazines*

I love this book!!!

This book focuses on the hugely complex issues of equity and inclusion, with a real razor sharp focus on the causes and consequences of what it is to be a disadvantaged student.

Where Matt gets it right is to focus on practical and simple solutions and he keeps the focus tight, honing in on the importance of attendance, positive behaviour and generating a community.

If you want a book that is brimming with practical advice, hints, tips and guidance from someone who actually does the job then this is the book for you. The secret is the author keeps it real!

What a gem of a read. Bravo!

– Sam Strickland, *Principal and CEO*

Matt's book series is a timely collection for UK based educators looking to level the playing field for disadvantaged students and 'build more equity in education'.

Matt's ABC framework provides a meaningful reference point to help cut through the complexities required to create an inclusive school culture. In addition, his framework will help schools to unpick institutional factors that prevent students from attending school.

No matter your stance in education, this book series is essential reading.

– Bukky Yusuf, *Leadership Development Coach*

Rooted in the realities of children's lives, this book from master story-teller Matt Bromley will prove invaluable in helping school leaders ask themselves hard but essential questions about equity and inclusion.

– Jean Gross CBE, *former government Communication Champion for children*

In this essential first volume of the *Equity in Education* series, Matt Bromley confronts one of today's most pressing challenges: building a culture of true inclusion and belonging in schools.

With a fresh look at educational disadvantage and the widening societal divide, Bromley offers practical, research-backed strategies to create environments where every student can thrive.

Anchored in real-world school experience, the book's straightforward ABC framework — Attendance, Behaviours, and Community — equips educators with actionable tools to address inequity head-on.

This is more than a call for change; it's a guide for educators ready to make a meaningful impact and challenges the misconception that we can do this alone with high expectations and zero tolerance approaches in schools.

– Sean Harris, *Director of People, Learning and Community Engagement, Tees Valley Education*

Why School Doesn't Work for Every Child neatly brings together the evidence and offers practical steps for those working on school priority areas such as attendance. This book reminds us to put learner and family experiences of school life at the forefront of our work, and to continuously reflect on our work on inclusion to ensure school works for every child.

– Kate Anstey, *Director of Education, the Child Poverty Action Group*

Why School Doesn't Work for Every Child

Every child, no matter their starting point or background and no matter their additional and different needs, should have an equitable chance of success at school.

This first book in the *Equity in Education* series looks at how schools can foster a better sense of belonging and ensure they are truly inclusive of all learners, thus mitigating the effects of an increasingly unequal, fractured society. To ensure a child's birth does not also become their life's destiny, Matt Bromley shows how an inclusive school culture can be created through a process that is as simple as ABC:

- **Attendance:** raising the attendance and punctuality of disadvantaged learners.

- **Behaviours:** helping students develop appropriate behaviours for learning so that they can conduct themselves positively and develop the skills needed to access an increasingly challenging curriculum.

- **Community:** building a community around learners by putting family first and engaging with parents as partners in the process of educating their child.

Offering actionable guidance and strategies that can be used to support school development plans, the book sets out the practical ways schools can create a collaborative culture in which all staff understand the importance of inclusion as well as the part they play in helping to achieve it. As such, it is essential reading for all teachers and school leaders who want to ensure that every child has an equitable chance of success at school and in later life.

Matt Bromley is an education journalist, author, and advisor with 25 years of experience in teaching and leadership, including as a secondary school headteacher and academy principal, further education college vice principal, and multi-academy trust director. Matt is a public speaker, trainer, initial teacher training lecturer, and school improvement advisor. He remains a practising teacher, currently working in secondary, FE, and HE settings. Matt writes for various magazines, is the author of numerous best-selling books on education, and co-hosts an award-winning podcast.

Equity in Education Series

Series Editor: Matt Bromley

Schools sometimes fail to talk to the lived experiences of disadvantaged and vulnerable children, as well as those with additional and different needs – and, because they do not feel included in the school's social and emotional environment and the academic curriculum, they do not feel it is for them. This exciting new series looks at how schools can remove barriers to belonging and ensure they include the excluded and mitigate the effects of an unequal, fractured society. The books offer strategies to help schools foster a whole-school ethos of equity and inclusion, tackle the many causes of disadvantage, foster a sense of belonging for all, plan an ambitious curriculum that's accessible to all, and prepare learners for future success.

Why School Doesn't Work for Every Child

How to Create a Culture of Inclusion and Belonging
Matt Bromley

For more information about this series, please visit: https://www.routledge.com/Equity-in-Education-Series/book-series/EIES

Why School Doesn't Work for Every Child

How to Create a Culture of Inclusion and Belonging

Matt Bromley

LONDON AND NEW YORK

Designed cover image: © Getty Images

First published 2025
by Routledge
4 Park Square, Milton Park, Abingdon, Oxon OX14 4RN

and by Routledge
605 Third Avenue, New York, NY 10158

Routledge is an imprint of the Taylor & Francis Group, an informa business

© 2025 Matt Bromley

The right of Matt Bromley to be identified as author of this work has been asserted
in accordance with sections 77 and 78 of the Copyright, Designs and Patents Act 1988.

All rights reserved. No part of this book may be reprinted or reproduced or utilised
in any form or by any electronic, mechanical, or other means, now known or hereafter
invented, including photocopying and recording, or in any information storage or retrieval
system, without permission in writing from the publishers.

Trademark notice: Product or corporate names may be trademarks or registered
trademarks, and are used only for identification and explanation without intent to
infringe.

British Library Cataloguing-in-Publication Data
A catalogue record for this book is available from the British Library

ISBN: 978-1-032-85947-7 (hbk)
ISBN: 978-1-032-85946-0 (pbk)
ISBN: 978-1-003-52063-4 (ebk)

DOI: 10.4324/9781003520634

Typeset in Gill Sans
by Apex CoVantage, LLC

Contents

List of figures	ix
Dedication and acknowledgements	xi
Introduction	1
1 A tale of two teens	8
2 Learner-led not label-led	13

Part I: A is for attendance

3 Attendance and disadvantage	21
4 Attendance policy	34
5 Attendance personalisation and practice	44
6 Attendance performance data and parents	57

Part II: B is for behaviours

7 Behaviour cultures	67
8 Behaviour classroom environments	76
9 Behaviour skills and consequences	88
10 Behaviours for learning	101
11 Behaviours for future success	110

vii

Part III: C is for community

12	Community and families first	127
13	Community cohesion and coherence	135
14	Community and the curriculum	144
15	Community and collaboration	156
16	Putting it all into practice	166
	Index	174

Figures

0.1	The ABC of school culture	5
1.1	Thomas and Tommy	8
2.1	Converting causes into consequences	14
3.1	Five factors linking disadvantage and attendance	26
3.2	The advantages of good attendance	28
3.3	The three-pronged approach to improving attendance	28
4.1	The 5Ps for improving attendance	34
5.1	Assess, plan, do, review cycle	46
7.1	Five elements of creating a culture of good behaviour	67
7.2	Creating the culture	68
7.3	Ingredients of a behaviour policy	70
7.4	Principles of a behaviour policy	71
7.5	Behaviour values	72
8.1	Features of a SEND classroom environment	79
8.2	Features of a growth mindset classroom	84
9.1	Seven classroom management strategies	91
9.2	Five behaviour management strategies	93
9.3	The graduated approach	95
9.4	Three layers of behaviour management	96
9.5	Reasons for misbehaviour	98
9.6	Strategies for making a success of a consequences system	99
10.1	Tips for developing self-efficacy	104
10.2	Avoiding learned helplessness	106
11.1	Elements of the personal development programme	110
11.2	Four ingredients in the recipe for success	114
11.3	Five study skills to explicitly teach	114
11.4	Types of motivation	117
11.5	The two dimensions of metacognition	120
11.6	The metacognitive cycle	121
12.1	Cornerstones of effective parental engagement	127
12.2	Features of effective parental communications	129
12.3	Six top tips for parental engagement	131
13.1	Three steps for bringing the community into the curriculum	138
13.2	Schema theory – three connections	139

13.3	The three purposes of extra-curricular activities	141
14.1	The 4Ps	144
14.2	Features of an inclusive curriculum plan	149
15.1	Ten classroom habits	160
16.1	Action plan	171

Dedication and acknowledgements

In this book, I espouse the importance of putting families first, so allow me to practice what I preach . . .

Firstly, I'd like to thank my wife, Kimberley, for her constant love and support. Thanks also to our children, Matilda, Amelia, and Harriet, and to my parents, Ray and Violet, and my in-laws, Dave and Karen.

I also argue in this book that it takes a village to raise a child and a community to educate one. This sentiment is true when writing a book, too. Although it can, at times, feel like a lonely pursuit, sitting solo at a computer trying – sometimes in vain – to populate a blank page, it is, in fact, a team sport. The words in this book may be my own, but the ideas behind them are far from it.

Secondly, therefore, I'd like to thank all the inspirational people – educators and academics, and parents and children – who I've worked with over the years and whose words and actions have filled my cup, percolated there awhile, then filtered into my thoughts.

Thirdly, I thank all those colleagues who have freely given their time to read and comment on this book and offer kind words of encouragement and praise. Thanks, too, to everyone at Routledge who has helped deliver this book into your hands.

This book is about making schools more inclusive places by fostering a better sense of belonging. It is about doing more for those who start with less so that a child's birth is not also their life's destiny.

And, therefore, my final dedication aptly goes to anyone who doesn't yet feel they belong and who doesn't yet know their place in the world. Whoever you are, wherever you come from: hold on; be strong. Your time will come, and you *will* find your way in the world. Life is unfair; society is unequal. You may have started the race further behind most of your competitors, and you may not be wearing the right running shoes on your feet. But keep going because you will reach that white tape and complete the race. It may take you longer, and the terrain may, at times, be tough, but persevere and be proud of who you are and what you do. If you falter, look left and right. You are not alone. We are here. We have got you. And together, we will help each other over the finish line. We are your tribe, and you belong right here.

Introduction

Broken Britain?

In 2024, in the UK, where I live and work, 4.3 million children were living in relative poverty – the highest number on record. 3.6 million children were living in absolute poverty, 2.2 million children were living in 'food insecure' households, and 820,000 were living in households that had resorted to using food banks. Four hundred thousand children had no beds of their own. Mental illness was on the rise, with one in four young people at the age of 17 having a mental illness, whilst 250,000 children had been denied help for mental health issues. Victorian diseases like malnutrition were returning, and life expectancy was falling. 3.2 million people were estimated to be in hygiene poverty, and too many parents were facing the impossible daily decision of whether to deny their children food or heating.

Perhaps unsurprisingly, the gap in attainment between disadvantaged and non-disadvantaged children had widened, and schools across the country were worried about a deterioration in learner attendance and behaviour.

Added to which, schools were experiencing an acute staff recruitment and retention crisis. A Department for Education report on the working lives of teachers and leaders published in spring 2022 showed that 56% of school staff thought their workload was unacceptable and that they did not have sufficient control over it, 25% said they were thinking of leaving the sector in the next 12 months for reasons other than retirement, and 61% were dissatisfied with their salary. Teacher wellbeing scores were lower than equivalent wellbeing scores for the UK population.

Over the course of the previous decade or so, I had seen my country become more divided. I had seen the gap between rich and poor grow, and the life chances of children from working-class backgrounds dwindle. For proof of this, just look at The Times Rich List. When the first rich list was compiled in 1989, a rich person had 6,000 times the average person. In 2024, it was 18,000 times.[1]

In fact, the chargesheet against the UK government of 2010–2024 makes for painful reading:

On jobs, workers in the UK suffered the longest and harshest pay squeeze in modern history.[2] They were £11,000 worse off a year after 15 years of "almost completely unprecedented" wage stagnation.[3]

DOI: 10.4324/9781003520634-1

On housing, in 2000, a home cost four times the average salary; by 2021, it had risen to eight times the average salary. Average monthly rental payments were 40% higher in 2024 than they were ten years earlier, while typical mortgage payments for the same properties were up 13%.[4]

On transport, spending on subsidies for bus and rail routes – where they are required to support 'socially necessary' routes – fell by 48% in real terms between 2009/10 and 2019/20, and spending on concessionary bus fares – a statutory duty that local authorities cannot ration – fell by 14%.[5] More than one in four bus services in England had been cut in the decade preceding 2024, and almost 5,000 bus routes have been axed since 2012, with the north-west and east of England the two regions worst affected.[6] In the decade to 2024, rail fares increased by 30%.[7]

On health, the NHS was chronically underfunded with the worst funding settlements in its history. The NHS was suffering the worst staffing crisis in its history, with nearly 112,000 full-time equivalent staff vacancies, including over 40,000 nurses.[8] NHS waiting lists to start elective care were at record levels in England – exceeding 7.4m – the highest since records began (August 2007).[9] Nearly five million patients each month in England had to wait more than a fortnight for a GP appointment.[10]

On energy, weekly road fuel prices have almost doubled since 2016,[11] and National Energy Action (NEA) calculated that 6.7 million people were living in fuel poverty.[12]

On Social Security, £14bn had been taken out of the welfare system since 2010/11.[13] For out-of-work families with two children, benefits covered less than half their costs – (48% for a couple, 49% for a lone parent) compared to more than 60% in 2012.[14] Working families had also lost out, with a £460 reduction compared to if the 2010 benefits system had still been in place.[15] In 2016, the Welfare Reform and Work Act abolished the Child Poverty Act, including the targets to reduce poverty. Between 2013 and 2022, the basic rate of unemployment benefits had lost value, leaving it at a 35-year low in real terms.[16]

Between 2008/09 and 2020/21, the number of foodbank users increased every year from just under 26,000 to more than 2.56 million.[17] In 2022/23, approximately 2.99 million people in the UK used a food bank.[18] 4.2 million children (or 29% of children) in the UK were living in poverty.[19]

On Local Authorities, the UK government reduced LA grants by £18.6bn (in 2019/20 prices) between 2009/10 and 2019/20, a 63% reduction in real terms.[20] Public spending cuts led to the closure of almost 800 libraries in the decade to 2024 – a fifth of the UK's total – and spending on libraries in 2009 was at £1 billion, but by 2019, it had declined by a quarter.[21] Freedom of Information requests to UK councils revealed 65 pools had closed, either temporarily or permanently, in the three years to March 2022.[22] Official figures show that 1,342 children's centres have closed over the last decade.[23] Local authority spending on youth services in England experienced a £1.1 billion cut in a decade.[24]

And finally, on education, school spending per pupil in England fell by 9% in real terms between 2009/10 and 2019/20, the largest cut in over 40 years.[25] The 2011 cut to the Educational Maintenance Allowance saw up to £30 a week taken away from 603,000 students from the poorest socio-economic groups.[26]

Although many of these issues are societal and not in the direct control of teachers and school leaders, it is important that we educators understand life outside our school gates and appreciate the daily challenges being faced by our learners. It is also important for us educators to do all we can to mitigate society's ills. I, therefore, make no apology for opening this book with a depressing picture of life in the UK today. But rest assured, in the remainder of this book, I will focus on what we can do to address the situation. And we can do so much. Educators are superheroes because we have the power to change lives and make the world a better place, one learner at a time.

I came from a poor, working-class background. Were it not for my schoolteachers – as well as access to local library and leisure facilities, a fairer system of social security, and a full government grant to pay for my university tuition fees and living expenses – I would not have succeeded at school, university, or in life. Knowing I was lucky, I have dedicated much of my working life to teaching in, leading, and now supporting schools in disadvantaged areas and to helping highlight and address inequalities in education. This four-book series has, therefore, been a lifetime in the making.

I must admit, I'm feeling more optimistic now than I was when I started writing the book because the goal of equity seems more achievable under a government that has acknowledged the need to transform the education system so that young people get the opportunities they deserve. There is now hope. Hope is not enough, of course, but it is a start. Together, though, we must convert hope into action. We must do something, not just say something.

I'm chair of a campaign called *Building Equity in Education,* which seeks to do just that. Our mission is "to use education as a lever for social justice by doing more for those who start with less to ensure a child's birth is not also their destiny".

I have written this book and the other three books in this series as an attempt to answer the question: how?

I want this book – and the three books that follow it – to be a practical guide to achieving equity in education and a set of strategies that schools can adopt to close the attainment gaps that have widened in recent years and to reverse social injustices.

About the series

This book is the first in a four-book series called *Equity in Education.* This book explores ways of creating a culture of equity and inclusion in our schools.

Equity in the education system has never been more important. As we have seen, we live in an increasingly unequal, fractured society, and schools, as microcosms of that society, are becoming increasingly unequal, fractured institutions. Schools cannot solve all of society's ills, of course, but they can do more to ensure a child's birth is not also their destiny.

Currently, disadvantaged children – whether that be those living in poverty, those from underrepresented cultures, ethnicities, and backgrounds, those with transient lives, or those with special educational needs and disabilities – start school behind their peers, and schools fail to close the gap. In fact, that gap widens as children travel through the education system, in part because knowledge begets knowledge: those children who start out behind find it harder than their peers to access the school curriculum and achieve, and thus, they fall further and further behind.

Covid exacerbated the problem. There's been a marked rise in absenteeism since the pandemic, and disadvantaged children are more than twice as likely to be persistently or severely absent as their peers, leading to lower progress, outcomes, life chances, and earnings power, not to mention poorer health and wellbeing. Disadvantaged children are more likely to experience mental health issues and struggle to study at home or access additional extra-curricular provisions.

The school curriculum often fails to talk to the *lived experiences* of disadvantaged children – and because they do not see themselves reflected in the school curriculum, they do not feel it is for them. Furthermore, they often lack the background knowledge and word power needed to access the full curriculum and so fail to achieve their potential.

It is not that these children are less able than their peers, nor that they do not exert the same amount of effort; it is the knowledge and skills gaps (what we might reductively call 'cultural capital') which result from their circumstances that pose a barrier to their success at school and then in later life.

This four-book series will explore ways of removing those barriers and providing a more equitable education to all; it will provide practical strategies to help schools *include* the *excluded* and mitigate some of the effects of an unequal, fractured society.

How the series is structured

Book 1 – the one you hold in your hands – is about creating a culture of inclusion and belonging. It explores ways of fostering a whole-school ethos of equity and fairness. On which, more in a moment.

Book 2 examines what this looks like in the classroom. It explores ways of tackling educational disadvantages of various kinds, including the socio-economic attainment gap, the gender and ethnicity attainment gaps, the SEND attainment gap, and other forms of vulnerability. And it offers practical strategies for achieving inclusive planning, teaching, and assessment.

Book 3 is about levelling the playing field for disadvantaged learners by planning the same ambitious curriculum for all, embedding high expectations for all, and ensuring high challenge with low threat.

Book 4 is about helping disadvantaged learners to become increasingly independent to prepare them for future success.

About this book

As I said previously, this book is about creating a culture of equity and inclusion in our schools.

As we will discover in the next chapter, the causes and consequences of disadvantage are complex. The solutions, therefore, are also complex. However, if we are to build more equity in education and ensure a child's birth does not become their destiny, then we must cut through this complexity and agree on a simple, logical approach. Cutting through complexity will allow us to communicate our approach to colleagues and our wider community and thus will help us gain traction and build a coalition. Cutting through complexity will also allow us to keep track of our progress and better diagnose what's working and what's not. It will help us to become more evidence-informed, proactive, and responsive.

The first task is to create an inclusive school culture, and to achieve this, I propose a process which is as simple as ABC:

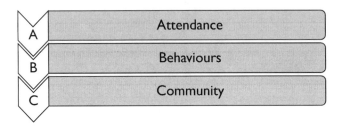

Figure 0.1 The ABC of school culture

As I say, the causes of educational disadvantage are complex; the way in which those causes manifest themselves in the classroom are equally complex, and, therefore, the solutions are complex. There are no silver bullets, no panaceas, no pills which one popped will proffer equity for all. There's more to building equity in education than my ABC for creating an inclusive school culture. Indeed, the subsequent books in this series will explore many of these additional factors. But we must start somewhere.

A is for attendance

It all starts with attendance because if learners are not attending school, or at least not regularly and on time, then we cannot help them engage with their education, learn, and make progress, and we cannot identify additional needs and put in place the appropriate support. Ensuring good attendance and punctuality must, therefore, come first.

Attendance is integral to building more equity in education because disadvantaged learners are more than twice as likely as their non-disadvantaged peers to be absent and persistently absent from school.

B is for behaviours

Once learners are attending, we need them to develop appropriate behaviours for learning. Note the plural 'behaviours' because this is two-fold:

- First, learners need to be helped to conduct themselves appropriately and to comply with our rules and expectations.
- Second, learners need to be helped to develop positive attitudes to learning and a raft of behaviours for learning so that they can access an increasingly challenging curriculum, actively engage with their studies, and make good progress.

- *Attitudes to learning* include being resilient and determined, having self-esteem and a belief in your ability to get better with hard work and effort, and having a plan for the future, which provides a source of motivation and a sense of purpose.

- *Behaviours for learning* take many forms but include study skills such as note-taking and independent research, debate and discussion, self- and peer-assessment, and metacognition and self-regulation.

C is for community

Once learners are attending and behaving appropriately and positively, we must focus on building a community around our learners by putting family first. We all know the adage that it takes a village to raise a child, but it also takes a community to educate one. Schools do not exist in isolation; they are a part of the community they serve.

The best schools reflect their local communities; they bring the community into their school and take learners out into that community. The best schools also look beyond their local communities and regard themselves as part of the national and international conversation. These schools teach learners how to be active members of their communities and how to be good citizens of the world.

Community is also about engaging with parents and families as partners in the process of educating their child, involving not just informing them on matters pertaining to their child's progress and wellbeing. Communication should be a dialogue, not a monologue, and be marked by dignity and respect. Our conversations should not apportion blame but ask how we can support parents to support their children.

Once we have achieved our ABC, the mark of success will be whether we have built a more equitable school, one which prepares all the young people we serve for their next steps in life. Do our learners leave school as well-rounded, cultured, inquisitive, caring, kind, resilient, knowledgeable human beings ready to make their own way in the world? And do we, therefore, make the world a better place?

How this book is structured

In the first chapter, we will explore a tale of two teens – two boys, Thomas and Tommy, from very different backgrounds whose success in school and in life is based not on their ability but on their birth. In Chapter 2, we will unpack the impact of their homelives on their educational experience, and I will advocate adopting a learner-led, rather than a label-led, approach to equity.

The remainder of this book is in three parts.

Part I is all about attendance. We will explore attendance and disadvantage, attendance policy, attendance personalisation and practice, and attendance performance data and parents.

Part II is all about behaviours. We will explore behaviour cultures, behaviour classroom environments, behaviour skills and consequences, behaviours for learning, and behaviours for future success.

Part III is all about community. We will explore community and families first, community cohesion and coherence, community and the curriculum, and community and collaboration.

So, without further delay, let's meet Thomas and Tommy . . .

Notes

1 https://gala.gre.ac.uk/id/eprint/42714/9/42714_TIPPET_The_good_life_at_the_top.pdf
2 https://www.tuc.org.uk/news/uk-set-worst-real-wage-squeeze-g7
3 https://www.theguardian.com/business/2023/mar/20/uuk-workers-wage-stagnation-resolution-foundation-thinktank
4 https://bmmagazine.co.uk/news/private-rents-in-uk-reach-record-highs-with-20-rises-in-manchester/
5 https://www.instituteforgovernment.org.uk/sites/default/files/publications/neighbourhood-services-under-strain.pdf
6 https://www.theguardian.com/politics/2022/apr/04/quarter-of-bus-routes-axed-in-england-in-last-decade
7 https://www.rmt.org.uk/campaigns/rail/paying-more-for-less/
8 https://www.kingsfund.org.uk/projects/nhs-in-a-nutshell/nhs-workforce
9 https://www.theguardian.com/society/2023/jun/08/nhs-chiefs-blame-staff-shortages-record-74m-people-waiting-lists-england
10 https://www.bbc.co.uk/news/health-65275367
11 https://www.theguardian.com/business/2022/aug/02/big-oil-profits-energy-bills-windfall-tax
12 https://www.bigissue.com/news/social-justice/fuel-poverty-in-the-uk-the-causes-figures-and-solutions/
13 https://neweconomics.org/2021/02/social-security-2010-comparison#:~:text=Changes%20to%20working%20age%20benefits,out%20the%20social%20security%20system.
14 https://cpag.org.uk/news-blogs/news-listings/full-time-workers-unable-reach-%E2%80%98no-frills%E2%80%99-living-standard-after-april%E2%80%99s
15 https://neweconomics.org/2021/02/social-security-2010-comparison
16 https://www.jrf.org.uk/press/main-out-work-benefit-sees-its-biggest-drop-value-fifty-years
17 https://www.statista.com/statistics/382695/uk-foodbank-users/
18 https://www.statista.com/statistics/382695/uk-foodbank-users/
19 https://www.actionforchildren.org.uk/blog/where-is-child-poverty-increasing-in-the-uk/
20 https://tribunemag.co.uk/2022/06/swimming-pools-closing-austerity-leisure-sport
21 https://tribunemag.co.uk/2021/01/the-quiet-disappearance-of-britains-public-libraries
22 https://www.bbc.co.uk/news/uk-62391323
23 https://questions-statements.parliament.uk/written-questions/detail/2022-06-23/23781
24 https://www.bigissue.com/news/politics/spending-cuts-decimated-public-services-since-2010-jeremy-hunt/
25 https://ifs.org.uk/publications/15588
26 https://researchbriefings.files.parliament.uk/documents/SN05778/SN05778.pdf

A tale of two teens

Figure 1.1 Thomas and Tommy

Thomas is 15. He lives with his mum and dad in a five-bedroomed detached house in leafy suburbia. When I visit, on a warm spring afternoon, cherry blossom carpets the driveway on which are parked two cars, one an SUV, the other a sleek and sporty saloon. I'm taken through a grand double-height hallway to a kitchen that boasts an island bigger than the SUV out front, and from there into the garden via bi-folding doors. Out back, there's a large summer house at the end of a manicured lawn. I spy a well-stocked bar and an industrial-looking barbecue grill. As I stare, Thomas's mum tells me that the *piece de resistance* is in the basement. Below stairs, she whispers somewhat conspiratorially; there's a home gym, cinema room, and – her eyes flick left then right – a heated swimming pool.

Tommy is also 15. Until recently, he lived with his mum and dad, but he and his mum were taken into emergency accommodation. Their temporary flat is on the other side of town. It is what an estate agent might call 'bijou'. It has one bedroom and one reception room. The reception consists of a kitchenette and a threadbare sofa, which is more spring than cushion. There is a shared bathroom down the corridor, which, I'm told, doesn't have a lock on the door or a shower over the bath. The carpets are sticky, and the whole building smells of damp. Tommy shares the bedroom, top-and-tailing with his younger sister; his mum takes the sofa. On the day I visit, it's raining outside, and the roof is leaking. The incessant drip-drip is distracting, like a head full of bees. Tommy's mum offers to take my coat and, when I decline, apologises for the

A tale of two teens **9**

lack of heating: the system is on the blink. It's fine, though; they're used to the cold; they hadn't been able to afford the heating bills at their old house.

Thomas is not yet home. His mum apologises. She tells me he plays tennis at the local club every Tuesday after school. In fact, he has quite a social life. Monday is chess club, Tuesday is tennis or squash, Wednesday is debating society, Thursday is piano, and Friday is time spent with friends. The weekends are no less frantic. Thomas plays rugby on Saturdays and spends Sundays online gaming. He is into computer games, his mum tells me, and has all the latest gear in his bedroom: a gamer's chair and desk, headset, multi-screen set-up, the works. He occasionally posts videos of himself playing games on YouTube and has picked up a big following. Since he monetised his channel, it's even started to pay. Thomas is putting the profits to one side to help fund a gap year after he's finished his A Levels. He wants to go to America and do Route 66, having seen a documentary about it on Netflix.

Tommy is also out when I call to see him. His mum isn't sure where he is but says he's probably on the estate somewhere. He hasn't yet made friends in the area, but he doesn't like to be in the flat, so he goes to the skate park or just hangs around the local shops. His mum thinks he's started vaping but hasn't talked to him about it yet. When he returns, Tommy tells me not to tell his mum, but he's never been to the stake park because he doesn't like the look of the other kids who hang out there. Instead, he was at a local Polish cafe because they have free Wi-Fi and don't ask questions as long as it's not too busy, and he sits quietly in a corner. He goes there often. It's warm and bright. There's a plug to charge his phone, and the tap water is free. I ask why he doesn't use the local library instead. He says there isn't one; it got closed down, just like the community centre where he used to live. Until the community centre closed, he would often go to the youth club there on Thursdays to use the computers or play sports.

When Thomas gets home, he's very apologetic about being late. He says his match went the full five sets, and the match point was thrilling. He's still buzzing from it. He says he will sleep well tonight. But first, he needs a shower and something to eat. I ask what he'll have. He says he knows there's some salmon left in the fridge, and he's been craving Eggs Royale all day. I ask if he's a good cook, and he says he's passable; Magda taught him how to cook a decent poached egg. He notes my look of confusion. Magda is the housekeeper, he explains. She comes in every day, cooks, cleans, that sort of thing. Part of the furniture. Part of the family, he means. So, tell me about your day, I say. Thomas tells me that school was okay. He gets too much homework, but it's not too hard. Mum and Dad help him with it whenever needed – and there's always his private tutor. Dad's good with maths and science and computing; mum is a linguist and can speak several languages. His mum works from home these days, so he is always on hand when needed; his dad runs his own business, so his time is his own. He organises his diary so he can pick Thomas up from the chess club and debating society and watch him play rugby at the weekends.

Tommy says his dad is a good man, but he lost his job in construction during Covid and struggled with the lockdowns. He became less patient and more prone to outbursts. He's a good man, Tommy repeats; he just doesn't know how to communicate and loses his temper more easily these days. Drinks too much, probably. Too much time to think, maybe. Tommy's mum works at the local supermarket and cleans at the hospital. She works shifts, which can be tough. Some days, Tommy gets his sister up and ready for school, and some days, he has to pick her up after school and babysit till Mum gets home. There's no washing machine in the flat, and the local launderette is expensive, so their clothes must survive several wears. I notice that Tommy's uniform is too small for him, and his trousers are muddy. How's school? I ask. Tommy shrugs. It's okay. Does he find it easy? The work's okay, he says. It's just that he struggles to concentrate and often feels tired, hungry, and distracted. He gets into trouble for not doing his homework or for daydreaming. He says he gets behind because he's often late. He has had run-ins with some other boys recently, too. He got detention but skipped it and is now worried about what they'll do to punish him. He knows what I'm thinking: yes, that's why he stayed away from school today; no, his mum doesn't know. Why did you skip detention? I ask. He tells me he had to pick his sister up after school and couldn't stay late. He didn't want the school phoning his mum at work. He worries she'll lose her job.

Thomas has easy manners and is confident and articulate. As he poaches an egg and picks at some sliced salmon, he chats to me about a story he saw on the TV news last night.

Tommy used to be eligible for free school meals. His mum doesn't know why that stopped; it has something to do with changes to her Universal Credit. All she knows is that they didn't suddenly get any richer! She tells me Tommy used to get extra help at school because of something called the Pupil Premium. That stopped, too. Again, she doesn't know why. She is quick to tell me they're not benefits cheats or scroungers. She works hard and has two jobs. She has always worked since she left school; she believes in paying her own way in life. She says she comes from a proud family of grafters and doesn't want hand-outs. But the bills have gone up lately. They can't afford to heat the flat, have to keep the lights off, and limit TV usage. But the kids never go hungry, she insists, albeit unconvincingly. She says food is so expensive these days, too. She blames Brexit. She wishes she hadn't voted for it, wishes she hadn't bought the lies writ large on the side of a bus. Said she thought she was helping the NHS; it turns out it's made matters worse. She knows they've cut staffing at the hospital where she cleans and that waiting lists are through the roof. She admits she sometimes uses the food bank but "don't tell the kids; they'd be so embarrassed".

Thomas intends to stay on at school to do his A Levels, then take a year out, travelling. After that, he wants to go to university to read Economics like his dad did. He says his dad can get him a job in the City and that he can take over the family business when he's earned his stripes. He knows what he needs to get in his GCSEs and what A Levels will be best for university applications. He knows all his extra-curricular activities will help when it comes to his UCAS form, too, and his parents have said they'll help him financially. I ask what his early childhood was like. Thomas tells me about family holidays – in the days before his dad bought a villa in Spain, they'd travel Europe. He has fond memories of camping by Lake Como during a storm, of touring the Nou Camp in Barcelona, and of visiting Ann Frank's house in Amsterdam. He says weekends were always busy – his parents liked to go to the theatre and to visit art galleries and museums. His mum is a bit obsessed with churches, he tells me. He's seen enough old buildings to last a lifetime. Books also feature heavily in his early memories. He says his dad would read to him most nights. His favourite author was Roald Dahl. The house has always been full of books.

Tommy says he's been feeling increasingly anxious. Anxious about school, about home-work, about getting into trouble; anxious about not sleeping, not eating; anxious about his appearance, his health, his sister, his mum, where they're going to live next, what's going to happen to his dad . . . I suggest asking the school to refer him for specialist support, all the while knowing the waiting list is somewhere north of two years. He says he doesn't need help; he's not mental, just worries a lot about a lot.

Thomas is a high-performing student and predicted a raft of grade 9s in his GCSEs next year. Tommy is not.

Thomas and Tommy are students at the same school.

Thomas and Tommy have the same IQ.

Diminishing the difference

Thomas and Tommy may be fictional, but their stories are far from unusual. You may think I've created caricatures, but I have met many young people like Thomas and Tommy in my quarter-century working in education. Their life stories are not exaggerated; indeed, I could have added other risk factors. Thomas could have been privately educated; Tommy could have been black or a Traveller, a looked-after child, a student with learning difficulties, or a physical disability.

But, even without these additional factors in play, Thomas and Tommy can teach us some important lessons about society and about our schools. I'll leave the social commentary to politicians, but let's consider what this means for schools.

Imagine you work at the school which both Thomas and Tommy attend. In fact, both boys are in your class. Your school operates a zero-tolerance approach to behaviour and has high expectations of all learners. Corridor and canteen conduct is highly regimented. Posters on the wall carry mnemonics instructing learners in every aspect of school life. Lessons follow a prescribed pattern: after silently entering the room and taking their seats, learners complete a 'do now' task which is already on the board. After the register is taken, there's a starter activity, and then the teacher introduces new content. Every learner is taught the same curriculum. Your school doesn't believe in dumbing down, in the soft bigotry of low expectations. Behaviour is not regarded as a form of communication; rather, it is the mark of a naughty child who needs strict rules and routine. The school operates as a meritocracy. Learners who attend on time and with the right equipment, behave well, consistently do all their homework to a high standard, always engage in lessons, answer questions articulately and in-depth, and volunteer for extra-curricular activities and leadership responsibilities are rewarded with prizes and praise. Those who do not are not.

Imagine that ability, aptitude, capability, or whatever you want to call it, is not a factor. Thomas and Tommy are equally gifted or equally average; you decide. Who would you put your money on receiving the most prizes and praise, making better progress, and leaving school with better outcomes, not only in terms of qualifications but also in their personal development and their preparedness for the next stage of their lives? Who, then, do you think is most likely to go on to post-16 study and then university? Who will find the better, higher-paid job? Who will enjoy better health and well-being for the rest of their lives? Who will live longer?

There's little doubt that Thomas will outperform Tommy at school and indeed at every juncture of their lives, not because he's brighter or harder working, but because he started the race halfway round the track and has more expensive running shoes.

You see, *it's not about ability* – a phrase I utter so often I think I'll get it printed on a tee shirt. Learners from socio-economic deprivation, or the working classes, are no less able than those from affluence and higher social status. Likewise, learners with SEND are no less able, nor are Black and ethnic minority learners. Instead, it is about an accident of birth. And sadly, a child's birth all too often becomes their destiny.

In seeking to achieve equity in education, we must not conflate advantage with ability. Think not that your disadvantaged learners are less able but that they have not been afforded the same opportunities as their more advantaged peers and thus have gaps in their knowledge and skills. Think not that your SEND learners have difficulties or disabilities but that the school environment is not suited to their additional needs, that their impairment becomes disabling because our expectations of how they engage in class and demonstrate their learning are not well-matched to their needs.

2 Learner-led not label-led

Converting causes to consequences

We often take a label-led approach in schools. In other words, our actions are driven by the label attached to a learner. For example, we see that a learner is a 'Pupil Premium[1] student' or a 'FSM[2] child' and assume that's all we need to know. We act on the label. For example, we:

- Mark all labelled learners' books first

- We seat labelled learners at the front of class

- We fund trips and resources for labelled learners

But a label-led approach is misguided on several counts:

1. It mistakes the label for an educational disadvantage

2. It assumes all learners with the same label are the same

3. It isolates or – worse – stigmatises learners with labels

Not every learner who has a label will need special treatment. Their 'accident of birth' may have no impact on their ability to access the same ambitious school curriculum as their peers and achieve in line with those peers. The reverse is also true: just because a learner does not carry a label does not mean they will not be educationally disadvantaged in some way. Also, not all learners with the same label will experience the same circumstances or suffer the same educational disadvantages – they are not a homogenous group, and the label can mask significant differences among the labelled cohort. What's more, the label tells you little about the educational disadvantage they might experience and, therefore, tells you little about what you can do to address the disadvantage.

Rather than follow a label-led approach, therefore, I'd recommend a learner-led approach. This is marked by:

DOI: 10.4324/9781003520634-3

13

14 Why School Doesn't Work for Every Child

- Giving targeted feedback to the learners most at risk of underachievement
- Targeting questions strategically to check learners' understanding
- Responsive teaching approaches to maximise learners' chances of success

Taking a learner-led approach is about converting the *causes* of disadvantage into tangible classroom *consequences*.

The causes might be:

Figure 2.1 Converting causes into consequences

- Living in a low-income home
- Experiencing high levels of mobility
- Having English as an additional language
- Special educational needs
- A mental or physical disability
- Coming from some ethnicities/cultures
- A long-term health condition
- Being a caregiver
- Contributing to family income
- Having a family member in prison
- Low levels of education in the family
- Being geographically isolated
- Being socially isolated
- Being supported by external agencies, including a social worker

The consequences might be:

- Gaps in vocabulary
- Limited literacy skills
- Limited numeracy skills
- Cognitive impairment

- Impaired language processing

- Gaps in background knowledge

- Attention deficiencies

- Low self-esteem

- Limited self-regulation skills

- Difficulties controlling emotions

- Low levels of motivation

- Limited social skills

- Low aspirations/awareness of future pathways

- Limited access to learning resources

- Low levels of support outside of school

Please note that neither of the lists presented previously is exhaustive.

Let's return to Tommy, whom we met in Chapter 1. What are the *causes* and *consequences* of Tommy's disadvantage?

The causes and consequences of Tommy's disadvantage

Tommy lives in poverty. His family struggled financially before Covid, but the impact of the pandemic *and* the cost-of-living crisis struck hard. His dad lost his job during the pandemic; his mum works two jobs for the minimum wage. Poverty begets poverty. Life costs more if you're poor. This is called the 'poverty premium'. According to the Joseph Rowntree Foundation (JRF), this may include "paying for energy through more expensive prepayment meters, which are used mainly by low-income households; paying more due to a lack of banking facilities for direct debit payments; paying more in fixed costs due to low consumption".[3] JRF goes on to explain that the "people in poverty are more likely to live in deprived areas, where home contents insurance premiums are higher".

In short, the poverty premium relates to a higher chance of paying a higher price, often associated with something related to poverty but not necessarily poverty itself. Further, "being in poverty may also mean lacking the resources to get around the problem – for example, the ability to afford transport to a supermarket rather than relying on higher-cost local shops".[4]

Poverty and cognitive function

Poverty also impairs cognitive function, making it more likely that someone with limited financial means will make bad decisions. This is, in part, because poverty-related concerns consume mental resources, leaving less for other tasks.

Children who grow up impoverished suffer from poor living standards, develop fewer skills for the workplace, and earn lower wages as adults.[5] Parents in poverty are less likely to be able to afford essentials for their children, such as food and heating. They're also less likely to be able to provide a decent standard of living or be able to allow their children to take part in enjoyable activities. Parents in poverty also face food insecurity and cramped living conditions. All these issues impact children's mental health.[6]

Tommy suffers from poor sleep hygiene for several reasons. Firstly, he shares a bed with his younger sister. Secondly, his home is cold. Thirdly, he is not eating enough, or at least not healthily. The stress of his new life, as well as worrying about school and family, are also likely to impair his sleep.

Tommy experiences hunger, and the food he does eat, because the source of food is limited, is often ultra-processed. He will probably lack energy as a result and will be storing up future health concerns. His hunger will impede his concentration and his behaviour. Although we may sometimes joke about being 'hangry', the link between hunger and anger is very real. Tommy will probably struggle to stay focused in class and to respond politely and diplomatically when he's challenged about it.

Poverty and mental health

Tommy's mental health is also declining. Tommy has no privacy. Tommy has few friends and none near his new home. He has no outlet for his emotions, no one to talk to or turn to for help or advice. He has no space to think. He is growing up too fast, looking after his younger sister and worrying about his mum and dad. He is frequently anxious about attending school and about the fact he struggles to complete his homework due to a lack of means *and* a lack of opportunity. He worries about his uniform and about being bullied for his unkempt appearance. He struggles in social situations and is likely to lack the social skills needed for future success.

Poverty and cultural capital

Tommy does not have access to extra-curricular activities that would help build his cultural capital, keep him fit and healthy, and develop his personal and emotional skills. Unlike Thomas, he cannot play sports beyond his weekly PE lesson. And when his PE kit has not been washed and smells, he must absent himself from that, even though he enjoys it. This impacts not only his physical health but also his socialisation, self-esteem, and motivation. Unlike Thomas, he cannot attend debating society, and this puts him at a distinct disadvantage when it comes to communicating with confidence and articulacy in various contexts. Since many people conflate ability or intelligence with confident communication, this will be an impairment when – if – Tommy is interviewed for college, university, or a job.

Tommy is unable to attend extra-curricular activities not only because he now lives further from his school and struggles with transportation and not only because he must collect his sister after school some days but also because he knows he cannot afford the additional cost of equipment and trips. Further, he is barred from attending some activities because they are regarded by his school as a reward for good conduct, and he has not accrued enough house points to qualify.

Tommy lacks *cultural capital*, not only because he cannot engage in extra-curricular activities or afford to go on school trips but also because his family cannot afford to take part in activities or take holidays. Tommy, unlike Thomas, has limited experience of "old buildings" or museums and art galleries, and he has never left the country, so he has no experience of foreign travel. His frame of reference is, therefore, much smaller, and as knowledge begets knowledge and the more you know, the easier it is to know more; this impairs his ability to learn new information in school. This phenomenon is known as The Matthew Effect: the rich shall get richer, and the poor shall get poorer. Learners who start school behind fall further and further behind as they travel through the education system because they don't have the foundational knowledge needed to access the curriculum and learn more.

Beyond the label

Although Tommy struggles at school, due to benefits reforms, he is no longer eligible for the Pupil Premium, and so his school, which is label-led, not learner-led, no longer targets him for additional support.

On the surface, Tommy's school sounds like the kind of place we'd want to send our own children and the kind of place we'd like to work. It's well-organised and highly structured. It espouses high expectations and prizes hard work and engagement. Learners like Thomas do well. But the school isn't working for the likes of Tommy. This is why we should judge schools by the outcomes they achieve for the most disadvantaged learners. And this is why we should build more equity in education.

Notes

1 The Pupil Premium is a grant given to schools in England to help close the attainment gap between disadvantaged learners and their peers. Learners are eligible for the additional funding if they claim free school meals, are or have been looked after by a local authority, or come from a service family.
2 Eligible for Free Schools Meals, a common measure of disadvantage.
3 https://www.jrf.org.uk/cost-of-living/poverty-and-the-cost-of-living
4 https://www.jrf.org.uk/cost-of-living/poverty-and-the-cost-of-living
5 https://www.unicef.org/social-policy/child-poverty
6 https://www.actionforchildren.org.uk/blog/how-poverty-affects-childrens-mental-health/

PART I
A is for attendance

3 Attendance and disadvantage

If they don't attend, they can't learn

If learners do not attend school, or at least not regularly and on time, then we cannot help them engage with education, learn and make progress, and achieve good academic outcomes, as well as social and emotional outcomes, that will mitigate their differences and disadvantages. Therefore, in our plight to build more equity in education, improving attendance must come first. That's why the A of my ABC of creating an inclusive school culture stands for attendance.

Since the Covid-19 pandemic, attendance in schools worldwide has plummeted.

In England, where I work, absence rates spiked after the national lockdowns, during which most learners were schooled at home, and rates have remained stubbornly high since then. Rates of persistent absence (defined as when a learner's overall absence equates to 10% or more of possible sessions) more than doubled after the pandemic, and they, too, have barely shifted since.

What's more, the 'attendance gap' – the difference in absence rates between disadvantaged learners and their non-disadvantaged peers – which has long been a problem, was stretched during the pandemic, with learners from disadvantaged backgrounds significantly more likely to be both absent and persistently absent than their peers. In fact, in England, data from the last few years shows that disadvantaged learners are, on average, more than twice as likely as their non-disadvantaged peers to be persistently absent.

Moreover, whereas persistent absence rates among non-disadvantaged learners have fallen since the pandemic, albeit only by tenths of a percentage point, persistent absence rates for learners from disadvantaged backgrounds have continued to worsen.

Attendance is intersectional. Learners with other risk factors, such as living in poverty, having special educational needs, having high levels of mobility, or coming from certain ethnicities or cultures, are more likely to struggle with their attendance and punctuality. Further, poor attendance is often a flag for another issue, including safeguarding.

A seismic shift?

A study by the think tank Public First[1] published in September 2023 found that there had been a "seismic shift" in parental attitudes to school attendance since Covid – a shift, they say, that

DOI: 10.4324/9781003520634-5

22 Why School Doesn't Work for Every Child

requires a monumental multi-service effort to change. They found that it was no longer the case that every day at school was seen to matter – at least from the perspective of parents.

In my experience of working directly with schools, I think this is due, at least in part, to the fact that parents were reassured that home-schooling during the Covid-19 lockdowns would not be detrimental to their child's education. And yet, evidence suggests the opposite is true. We are still seeing the long shadow of Covid: more children are experiencing mental health problems, including anxiety,[2] more children are struggling with their social and emotional development,[3] and academic outcomes have fallen and are predicted to continue to fall over the next few years.[4] Not attending school in-person during the lockdowns should have under-lined the importance of school attendance, not undermined it. The first task before us, then, if we are to improve attendance, is to reverse this narrative, to tackle the paradox. **Parents need to know that every day counts**.

Breaking the social contract

The Public First report also found that there had been a fundamental breakdown in the rela-tionship between schools and parents across the socio-economic spectrum. This, I think, reflects a wider problem: a breaking of the social contract between citizens and the state. Fewer people now trust the state or respect its authority. We need not look far to under-stand why this might be the case. In the UK, Boris Johnson, the prime minister at the time of the Covid lockdowns, was found to have lied, including about attending parties in Number 10 whilst the electorate obeyed the social distancing rules he espoused nightly. Many people grieved alone at the loss of loved ones.

Sadly, many parents regard schools as an instrument of the state and thus have less trust in and respect for the authority of schools than was the case pre-pandemic. Indeed, Amanda Spielman, in her final annual report as head of the schools' inspectorate in England, said that "in education we have seen a troubling shift in attitudes since the pandemic. The social contract that has long bound parents and schools together has been damaged".[5]

This might also help explain why term-time holidays are now much more socially acceptable across all socio-economic groups. Before the pandemic, some low-income families regarded the risk of a fixed penalty notice as preferable to the additional cost of vacationing during the school holidays. Now, say Public First, parents from across the social strata are willing to take their children out of school for a holiday. This is, in part, linked to my previous points, but it also speaks, I think, of some parents' belief, post-pandemic, that holidays are an educational experience that can build cultural capital as well as a way to repair the damage to a child's personal development reaped by Covid.

Draconian systems?

Public First concluded that school-level attendance systems felt increasingly draconian to fami-lies and yet not sufficiently robust or accurate. Likewise, sanctions were seen as both irrelevant and antagonistic across all parent groups. Certainly, I think there is little value in sharing headline statistics with parents. Attendance statistics are often meaningless and certainly do not have the traction we might think. Further, many parents regard school communications on attendance to be too generic — not related to their child — and often negative. Indeed, in my experience, schools do tend to adopt a deficit model, talking of absences and lateness rather than attendance and punctuality and about the detrimental impact of missing school rather than about the positive benefits of good attendance. **Schools need to flip the conversation.**

Factors affecting attendance

Further to the Public First report, an article in *The Guardian* newspaper by Sally Weale,[6] published on 28 June 2023, sought to headline the factors affecting school attendance. The article cited seven such factors. Here, I will explore the most pertinent five:

Anxiety and mental health issues

The Guardian said:

> While poor mental health among young people was a growing concern before the pandemic, it has deteriorated since. According to NHS Digital, 18% of children aged seven to 16 had a probable mental disorder in 2022, up from 12.1% in 2017, meaning already overstretched NHS mental health services are unable to cope with rising demand.[7]

In my experience, there are several factors at play. Firstly, during Covid lockdowns, a majority of children were not attending school in-person, so mental health needs were not being routinely identified and diagnosed contemporaneously. When learners returned to school in-person following the lockdowns, there was, therefore, a spike in the number of children being identified as potentially having mental health issues and being referred to NHS services for diagnosis and support. Coupled with this, more children began to experience poor mental health as a direct result of the lockdowns, increasing the size of that spike. Further, there was an increase in the number of parents experiencing poor mental health as a result of the lockdowns, and some parents now struggle to ensure their child attends school either because they do not have the capacity to do so or because they choose to keep their child at home for support. And underscoring all of this is the fact that the NHS has suffered funding cuts and cuts to its workforce. The result of all these factors combined is that there is a serious lag from referral to a child being seen by a mental health specialist. In many of the schools I work with, that lag is about two years. We can assume that, during those two years, some children will vote with their feet, deciding that school is simply not an option.

Poverty

The Guardian said:

> Deprivation and poverty have always been barriers to school attendance, but the upheaval caused by Covid and the cost-of-living crisis that followed has resulted in many more families struggling. . . . Given a choice of food or school, food wins.[8]

Again, I know the truth of this from my direct work with schools. Poverty is crippling. We saw some of its effects in Tommy's story. The proportion of children living in poverty has increased markedly since 2010. Take, for example, the number of children living in poverty with at least one working parent, which increased by 44% between 2010 and 2023, the equivalent of 1350 more children being dragged into poverty every week. Analysis by the Trades Union Congress (TUC) shows that, in 2023, there were three million children in working households living below the breadline in the UK.[9] The TUC says that "a 'toxic combination' of wage stagnation, rising insecure work and cuts to social security have had a devastating impact on family budgets". Added to this is an increase in the cost of living, not least in the price of energy. According to an analysis by the House of Commons Library in March 2024, "typical household energy bills increased by 54% in April 2022 and 27% in October 2022", and although "lower wholesale prices have [since] led to falls in prices, bills remain around 59% above their winter 2021/22 levels".[10] This has resulted in "around 4 in 10 adults (41%) who pay energy bills [saying it is now] very or somewhat difficult to afford them" and "around one in five (19%) adults [reporting] that they were occasionally, hardly ever, or never able to keep comfortably warm in their home", according to the Office for National Statistics.[11]

Many more children now live in cold, cramped, damn accommodation without adequate heating and lighting, let alone broadband internet and access to a device. These children are likely to experience poor sleep hygiene and poor nutrition. They are more likely to experience difficulties buying school uniforms and keeping their uniforms clean and in good repair. They are also more likely to experience difficulties keeping themselves clean.

Taken together, poverty makes it much harder for children to get up on time, get dressed and breakfasted, and get to school – let alone to arrive at school having completed their homework to a good standard and feeling attentive, engaged, and motivated to learn.

Housing

The education charity School-Home Support,[12] which works with persistently absent learners and their families to improve school attendance, says that insecure, poor-quality housing is increasingly a barrier to children going to school.

The Guardian cites families who are moved into refuges because of domestic violence or into emergency accommodation after eviction as being particularly disadvantaged, finding themselves long distances from their child's school, making journeys expensive.

Coupled with what I said previously about the impact of poverty, many more children – including those who do not live in poverty – now live in unsuitable accommodations. Government figures published in April 2024 show nearly 112,000 households were in temporary accommodation on 31 December 2023, a 12.1% increase from the previous year. Of those, 63% included dependent children, hitting record levels in 2023.[13] Fifty-five children without a permanent home died in temporary accommodation in the four years to April 2024. An analysis of the National Child Mortality Database shows an additional 21 deaths in temporary accommodation since April 2019, up from the 34 deaths in homeless shelters previously stated.[14]

Once again, I hear of children now living too far from school to be able to afford or source transportation and others whose accommodation is wholly unsuitable and a barrier, not only to their education but also to their health.

Illness

Understandably, the pandemic took a heavy toll on learner absence as children contracted the virus. But, as well as absence as a result of being sick with Covid, lots of children missed out on social mixing during the lockdowns, and so did not get the same exposure to common germs as previous generations. This has likely made them more susceptible to illness since, which has further contributed to increases in absenteeism.

Most absences from school are caused by illness. But, in my experience, although there has indeed been a spike in the number of seasonable infections and viruses, children are now more likely than was the case pre-pandemic to be kept off school for minor illnesses. This is, in part, due to the fear that spread during the pandemic and a more cautious approach being taken, but also because more parents work from home or have hybrid working patterns and do not need to take time off to nurse a sick child. Likewise, when a parent can work from home, it is sometimes easier to allow a truculent child to stay at home rather than face a daily battle.

To tackle this, schools need to communicate with parents and arm them with the intelligence needed to make informed choices about whether to send their children to school or not. We'll come back to this shortly.

Special educational needs and disabilities

The Guardian said

> [I]t is well known that children with special educational needs and disabilities are more at risk of absence from school, and that link has become more pronounced since the pandemic, which took a particularly heavy toll on many of these pupils.[15]

The Children's Commissioner has suggested that "while some children [are] unable to attend because of healthcare appointments", more often they stay away "because the school [is] unable to deliver the required adjustments or provide a suitable learning environment".[16]

Like the mental health crisis, the cost-of-living crisis, and the housing crisis, SEND is a risk factor which intersects with attendance. Children with SEND are far more likely to absent themselves from school if they feel the environment is not suitable for them and that they do not belong. In short, if schools are not making reasonable adjustments to ensure that a child's additional needs are not barriers to their learning, then they are guilty of indirect discrimination under the Equality Act 2010.

To improve the attendance of children with SEND, therefore, we need to ensure we make effective use of adaptations and interventions, and we need to move from equality to equity, doing more and different things for those who start at a disadvantage to make education more accessible. This talks about the 'push' and 'pull' factors of school – what pushes learners away from school and what might pull them into school. We'll return to this soon.

Disadvantage and attendance

As I said previously, disadvantaged learners are more than twice as likely to be absent from school as their non-disadvantaged peers. Here is a summary of the top five factors that lead to lower attendance among disadvantaged learners:

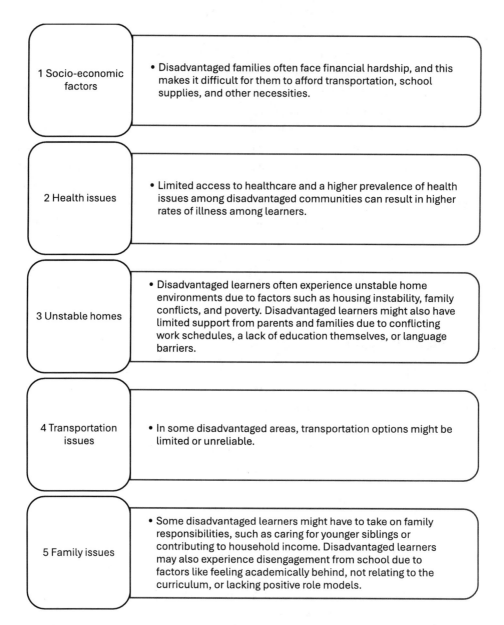

Figure 3.1 Five factors linking disadvantage and attendance

How can we address the attendance gap?

To narrow the attendance gap – that is to say, to break the link between disadvantage and absenteeism, I'd suggest we adopt the following mantras in our schools:

1. Every day counts

As we have seen, it is no longer the case that every parent regards every day at school as being important. We need to reverse this perception. We need to convince learners and their families that school is the best place to be, both in terms of being supported and protected and in terms of learning, making progress, and achieving good outcomes that will open doors to future success. We need to explain the importance of curriculum sequencing and show how difficult it is to catch up on lost learning. We need to show learners and families that school is about so much more than an education, vital though this is. We need to talk about the social and emotional development a child is afforded by attending school. And we need to talk about the life skills acquired at school.

2. Attendance is everyone's business

It's commonly accepted that safeguarding is everyone's business, but attendance should also be of concern to everyone working in a school, not least because it is so inextricably linked to safeguarding. Everyone in school has a part to play in promoting the benefits of good attendance and punctuality, as well as being alert to learner absences and lateness. All staff need to know the contents of the school's attendance policy and need to know what part they are expected to play in translating that policy into practice. All staff need training on the causes of absenteeism and on how to have sensitive conversations around attendance and punctuality. Those staff responsible for taking registers need training on how to use the system, including which codes to use and when, and how to follow up on any unexplained absences. Staff who are responsible for analysing attendance data – including identifying patterns and trends – need the skills to do so, and those with specific responsibilities around attendance improvement efforts and parental engagement need the skills necessary to undertake these duties effectively. In short, all staff needs to know that attendance is part of their job description, and there needs to be a planned programme of professional development in place to ensure that all staff can dispense their duties effectively.

Flip the conversation

Next, once we've adopted these two mantras, I'd suggest we flip the conversation and promote the benefits of good attendance. In practice, and as I said earlier, this means avoiding the deficit model approach whereby we talk about absences and lateness and share headline attendance statistics, which are often meaningless to parents. For example, to us, 85% attendance is a real cause for concern, but to many parents, it is not. After all, if we got 85% in a test, we'd probably pass and be pleased with ourselves. The headlines don't have the traction we might think, nor does talking about the adverse impact of absences or threatening sanctions. Rather, we should talk positively about the significant advantages afforded to learners who do attend regularly. And there are many advantages:

I'll explore these in more detail later.

Figure 3.2 The advantages of good attendance

A three-pronged approach

In tackling the 'attendance gap', once we've adopted those two mantras and flipped the conversation, I'd suggest we take a three-pronged approach which starts by exploring in-school factors – the push and pull of school life. In other words, what aspects of our school push some learners away, and what aspects might pull them back in? Only when we've explored ways of improving the school experience can and should we explore factors outside of school. This mindset should also govern the way we communicate with parents and families – rather than blaming parents for their child's absence from school or asking parents what *they* can and should do to address attendance issues, we should ask what *we* can do to support parents in getting their child into school.

The three prongs are as follows:

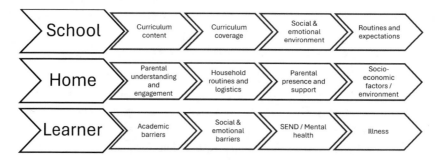

Figure 3.3 The three-pronged approach to improving attendance

I'll pose some self-evaluation questions for each of the previously mentioned factors now, but rest assured, we'll come back to all these factors in more depth through the course of this four-book series on *Equity in Education*.

School-based factors

Curriculum content

- To what extent do your curriculum content choices reflect your learners' lived experiences? Do they see themselves reflected in *what* you teach?

- To what extent do the examples you use to teach the curriculum – the case studies, models, illustrations, texts, etc. – represent your learners? Do they see themselves reflected in *how* you teach?

- Does your curriculum act as both a mirror – reflecting your learners' own lives and experiences to make it accessible – and a window – showing learners a world beyond their own lives and experiences to foster greater understanding?

Curriculum coverage

- Do you plan an ambitious, broad, and balanced curriculum that gives learners access to the best that has been thought and said and that represents excellence in each subject discipline?

- Do you give equal access to every learner to the same ambitious curriculum, regardless of starting point and additional and different needs, rather than dumbing it down?

- Do you ensure that all learners can access the same ambitious curriculum by diagnosing additional needs and converting the causes of disadvantage into tangible classroom consequences? Do you then help learners to overcome those barriers through adaptive teaching and interventions?

Social and emotional environment

- Do you foster a culture of inclusivity, respect, and tolerance? Do you understand the difficulties some learners might have with navigating your school environment, and do you make reasonable adjustments for them?

- Do you explicitly teach social and emotional development as part of your PSHE programme and across the curriculum to equip learners with the skills needed to engage positively with others and manage their emotional responses? Do all the adults who work in your school model healthy social and emotional skills?

- Do you have robust systems in place for preventing bullying and harassment and for tackling incidences of bullying when they do occur? Do learners feel safe and supported?

Routines and expectations

- Have you agreed on a set of social norms for your school – 'the way we do things around here'? Do you communicate and practice these daily routines so that they become automatic for all learners all the time?

- Are your expectations of learner behaviour clear and consistent, and do you repeatedly reinforce them? Are those expectations achievable for all learners, including disadvantaged learners and learners with additional needs? If not, do you make reasonable adjustments to them?

- Do you have an effective system of consequences which recognises learners who routinely meet your expectations and sanctions those who repeatedly and avoidably flout your rules and routines?

Home-based factors

Parental understanding and engagement

- Do you provide parent information sessions and share other forms of information to help parents and families understand the importance of education and the part they can play in supporting their child's education? Do you repeatedly signpost the value of education and offer practical suggestions to help parents engage with their child's learning, including helping with homework?

- Do you engage with parents as partners in the process of educating their child, involving them, not just informing them? Is parental communication a two-way process? Do you report back to parents on the actions you've taken in response to their feedback so that they know they have an important voice?

- Do you think innovatively about engaging parents who are harder to reach, including by meeting parents off-site at a neutral community venue and by enlisting other parents or community leaders to act as conduits of information for those parents who are reluctant to liaise with school staff?

Household routines and logistics

- Do you seek to understand what logistical barriers some families face to securing good attendance for their children? Do you explore practical solutions to overcome these barriers, such as sharing proven morning habits with all parents?

- Do you seek to understand issues around transportation and use discrete funding to help those in need access suitable transport? Do you work with your local authority and transport companies to find long-term solutions, including for those learners who are moved into accommodation further from school?

- Do you mitigate the problems some learners face at home in relation to their morning and after-school routines? For example, do you provide a breakfast club for those who would benefit from not only being fed but also from accessing help with uniforms and equipment before school starts? Do you provide homework clubs after school staffed by trained colleagues which provide access to a warm, safe environment and IT equipment to help those learners who do not have these advantages at home? Do you provide food and water at homework clubs? Do you ensure learners can access transport home afterwards?

Parental presence and support

- Do you make sure parents know about their legal obligations with regards to their child's attendance at school, and do you support them to make good decisions about their children? Do you promote the benefit of attendance in every interaction and ensure parents know where to go for help?

- Do you run – or signpost to – parent education classes which help equip families with the skills and strategies they need to provide a suitable home for their children? Does this include modelling healthy morning routines? Do you help parents to have difficult conversations with their children and to challenge inappropriate behaviours? Do you, for example, educate parents about ensuring their child stays safe online and manage screen time effectively?

- Do you talk about the value of education and encourage respected community figures to do likewise? Do you link educational outcomes to future life chances and to better health and wellbeing?

Socio-economic factors

- Do you *poverty-proof* your school, including by reducing the cost of school uniforms and running a used uniform service and by providing funded access to educational trips and extra-curricular activities?

- Do you provide access to resources such as food, clothing, and stationery for learners who live in poverty? Do you provide a safe and supportive environment in which learners who lack resources at home can complete homework and access help?

- Do you work with parents in a non-judgemental way to understand the impact poverty has on their ability to support their child's education, and do you provide access to help, including signposting external agencies? Do you help provide affordable transport? Do you ensure funding such as the Pupil Premium is spent where there is greatest need and where it will have the biggest impact rather than only spending it on those children who are eligible?

Learner-based factors

Academic barriers

- Do you diagnose learner starting points, including levels of literacy and numeracy, and put in place effective adaptations and interventions to help fill gaps in prior knowledge, including in vocabulary?

- Do you audit access to extra-curricular activities to ensure those in most need of opportunities to build their cultural capital are prioritised, targeted, and funded?

- Do you run a planned programme of professional development for teachers and teaching assistants that ensures all staff understand learners' needs and have a raft of strategies at their disposal to help scaffold those needs? Do you then monitor the impact of such strategies and ensure gaps are closing?

Social and emotional barriers

- Do you provide an effective programme of personal development which actively teaches learners social and emotional skills, including how to stay mentally healthy and cope with difficult situations?

- Do you have systems in place to ensure learners with social and emotional difficulties are identified in a timely manner and are offered support? Do you have a range of support strategies in place, including mentoring, access to specialist services, and robust systems for tackling bullying and harassment?

- Does your approach to behaviour management make learners feel safe and supported? Do you foster a collaborative environment and actively teach learners how to manage their emotions and work with others? Do you make reasonable adjustments for learners with social, emotional, and mental health needs to ensure they feel included and able to navigate friendships and make positive contributions to school life?

SEND and mental health

- Do you explicitly build a safe, calm, and supportive school culture and repeatedly reinforce social norms? Do you ensure your environment is not a barrier to learners with SEND by making reasonable adjustments? Do all learners feel they belong?

- Do you ensure your curriculum talks to learners' lived experiences, including reflecting the lives of learners with SEND and those with mental health issues? Do you actively teach tolerance and empathy and ensure other learners are respectful towards learners with SEND and learners with mental health issues?

- Do all staff model resilience and self-regulation? Do all staff have high expectations of learners with SEND and avoid perpetuating learned helplessness?

Illness

- Do you educate parents about what is too ill for school, including by sharing the NHS resource? Do you help parents make informed decisions, including by encouraging them to send their child to school if in doubt? Do all staff understand what is and is not 'ill enough' to warrant an absence from school? Do they challenge absences for more minor illnesses?

- Do you monitor trends in school-level illnesses and compare these to regional and national data? Do you promote good health, including by teaching learners how to stay physically and mentally healthy and by teaching learners about healthy eating?

- Do you educate learners and parents about mental health, making clear the difference between anxiety as a medical diagnosis and being generally apprehensive about school? Do you 'normalise' worrying about stressful or unfamiliar situations as a natural – and sometimes welcome – part of life?

Notes

1 Burtonshaw, S., & Dorrell, E. (2023). *Listening to, and learning from, parents in the attendance crisis*. Public First. https://www.publicfirst.co.uk/wp-content/uploads/2023/09/ATTENDANCE-REPORT-V02.pdf

2 https://www.ox.ac.uk/news/2023-09-21-young-people-s-mental-health-deteriorated-greater-rate-during-pandemic-major-new

3 https://educationendowmentfoundation.org.uk/news/new-pandemic-adversely-affected-young-childrens-development-with-fewer-reaching-expected-levels-by-the-end-of-reception-class

4 https://www.theguardian.com/education/2024/apr/24/pupils-in-england-facing-worst-exam-results-in-decades-after-covid-closures-says-study

5 https://www.gov.uk/government/publications/ofsted-annual-report-202223-education-childrens-services-and-skills/the-annual-report-of-his-majestys-chief-inspector-of-education-childrens-services-and-skills-202223#hmci-commentary

6 https://www.theguardian.com/education/2023/jun/28/covid-poverty-pupil-absence-england-schools-social-economic-pandemic-families

7 https://www.theguardian.com/education/2023/jun/28/covid-poverty-pupil-absence-england-schools-social-economic-pandemic-families

8 https://www.theguardian.com/education/2023/jun/28/covid-poverty-pupil-absence-england-schools-social-economic-pandemic-families

9 https://www.tuc.org.uk/news/tuc-child-poverty-working-households-has-increased-over-1300-week-2010#:~:text=The%20analysis%20shows%20that%20the,the%20breadline%20in%20the%20UK

10 https://commonslibrary.parliament.uk/research-briefings/cbp-9491/

11 https://www.ons.gov.uk/economy/inflationandpriceindices/articles/costoflivinginsights/energy

12 https://www.schoolhomesupport.org.uk/

13 https://www.gov.uk/government/statistics/statutory-homelessness-in-england-october-to-december-2023/statutory-homelessness-in-england-october-to-december-2023

14 https://new.basw.co.uk/about-social-work/psw-magazine/articles/housing-crisis-claiming-childrens-lives-according-shock

15 https://www.theguardian.com/education/2023/jun/28/covid-poverty-pupil-absence-england-schools-social-economic-pandemic-families

16 https://assets.childrenscommissioner.gov.uk/wpuploads/2023/02/cc-response-to-persistent-absence-inquiry.pdf

4 Attendance policy

Introducing the 5P framework

When I work with schools on improving attendance, I usually share the 5P framework I've developed. This process is designed to support a school's self-evaluation of existing attendance management procedures and to identify missed opportunities and new approaches. The 5Ps are:

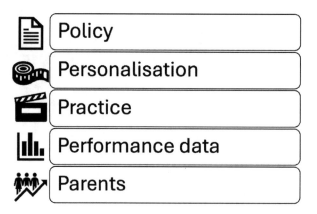

Figure 4.1 The 5Ps for improving attendance

In this chapter, I'm going to take you through the first P in the process: policy. In Chapter 5, we'll explore personalisation and practice. And in Chapter 6, we'll consider performance data and the part parents can play. As you work through each of the 5Ps, I'd suggest you conduct a self-evaluation for your school. The order is important – work through the process from start to finish. You might find the following action plan helpful for capturing your key takeaways:

Area of attendance practice	Current strengths How we know	Current areas for improvement How we know	Actions required What, who, when, how	Intended outcomes What success will look like
1 Policy				
2 Personalisation				
3 Practice				
4 Performance data				
5 Parents				

1 Policy

The first P in my 5P framework is policy because attendance improvement starts with policy. A school must have a clear policy that sets out its expectations of attendance and punctuality and explains the procedures that it will follow whenever a learner does not attend or is late for school and/or lessons.

However, a policy is of no use if it remains no more than a document locked in a dusty drawer; rather, it must be widely known and understood. The best way to achieve this is to consult on its contents with as wide an audience as possible. Invite contributions from staff, parents, external agencies, the local community, employers, and so on.

Once the policy has been consulted upon and agreed upon, it needs to be communicated as widely and as often as possible. We could, for example, include relevant segments of the policy in letters home and make it easily accessible via the school website. We could distribute it to new parents through transition materials, enrolment packs, and information evenings.

Having a policy that is known and understood is only half the battle won, though: it must then be put into practice, and this means ensuring it is known by staff and followed consistently by all staff and for all learners.

One tangible example where a policy is key is punctuality. The policy should stipulate what we regard as being late. Is it 1 minute, 5 minutes, or 10 or 15 minutes after the bell has tolled? Are learners classed as being on time if they attend before the register is closed? Is our definition of late the same for the statutory morning and afternoon register as for each lesson of the day? Whatever definition we decide upon and include in our policy must be adhered to by all staff all the time. Inconsistency in the application of attendance and punctuality procedures will sound the death knell.

Consistency is needed in the use of attendance codes, too. Staff need to know what code to use for different types of absences, and this should be clearly stipulated in the policy.

I'd suggest any policy review starts with a restatement of the law. The law is very simple, and all stakeholders – staff, learners, parents – need to know their legal duties in relation to attendance and why attendance is of such import that it is set down in statute.

The law entitles every child of compulsory school age to an efficient, full-time education suitable to their age, aptitude, and any special educational need they may have. It is the legal responsibility of every parent to make sure their child receives that education either by attendance at a school or by education other than at a school. Where parents choose to have their child registered at school, they have an additional legal duty to ensure their child attends that school regularly. This means their child must attend every day that the school is open, except in a small number of allowable circumstances, such as being too ill to attend or being given permission for an absence in advance from the school. This is because the learners with the highest attainment at the end of key stage 2 and key stage 4 have higher rates of attendance over the key stage compared to those with the lowest attainment. Further, for the most vulnerable learners, regular attendance is also an important protective factor and the best opportunity for needs to be identified and support provided.

A key aspect of improving attendance is to articulate the positive benefits of attendance.

I set out some of the advantages of good attendance earlier. For example, I said that learners with good attendance make better progress in school and achieve stronger outcomes. This enables learners to progress to further and higher education and secure jobs with higher earnings potential. Good attendance also increases the chances of a learner enjoying good health and wellbeing.

To help you share the tangible benefits of good attendance with your learners and their families, here's my top 3:

1. **Academic outcomes:** Good attendance helps learners stay engaged in their learning and ensures they don't miss out on important lessons. Missing lessons can lead to gaps in understanding, making it harder for learners to keep up. There is no substitute for being present in class when content is first taught and class debates and discussions are had. Furthermore, there is no substitute for having access to a teacher: attending classes regularly allows learners to receive individualised help and clarification when needed. Furthermore, most subject disciplines are accumulative; they build layer upon layer of knowledge. New knowledge is learned within the context of prior knowledge; and connections are made that form ever more complex schema in long-term memory. If learners frequently miss lessons, they are likely to struggle to grasp new concepts because they lack the foundational understanding that was covered in their absence.

2. **Social skills and self-esteem:** Classroom interactions don't just lead to learning; they also contribute to a deeper understanding of the world. Learners who attend regularly have more opportunities to ask questions, participate in discussions, and collaborate with their peers. Since school is not just about acquiring academic knowledge, good attendance also provides access to an environment where learners can learn important social skills, teamwork, and cooperation. Good attendance allows young people to build relationships with their peers and develop social confidence. Furthermore, good attendance helps establish healthy and handy routines, thus helping learners develop good time-management skills and discipline. These skills are valuable throughout life, whether in education, work, or personal activities.

3. **Preparation for life:** Classroom assessments are designed to gauge a learner's understanding of curriculum content. Learners who attend regularly are better prepared for these assessments and receive feedback that helps them make further, faster progress. Good attendance habits in school can also translate into good attendance habits in the workplace

and other areas of life. Punctuality and reliability are highly valued qualities by employers and in various life situations. Conversely, learners with poor attendance are more likely to fall behind and become disengaged from their studies, increasing the risk of future failure. School is also the best place for additional needs to be identified and diagnosed and for vulnerable learners to be protected. What's more, a positive school experience contributes to a learner's overall well-being: active participation in school activities, social interactions, and learning experiences can have a positive long-term impact on mental and emotional health.

Returning to the law, parents are expected to ensure their child attends school every day it is open, except if their child is too ill to attend. This rather begs the question, what is 'too ill'?

Many parents struggle to make informed decisions about this, and there has been an increase in the number of children being kept off school for minor illnesses post-pandemic. To help parents make better decisions, therefore, schools can offer guidance. This guidance is, I think, two-fold. Firstly, we should offer advice on what symptoms necessitate a child staying away from school and which symptoms do not. Secondly, we should offer to help make the decision by recommending that parents bring their child to school if they are in any doubt about whether they are fit to attend. This is particularly helpful if you have a school nurse or medical practitioner working on-site.

There are two useful resources I'd suggest sharing with parents to help them make good decisions about whether to send their child to school or not:

1. **The NHS 'Is my child too ill for school' advice, which can be found at**
   https://www.nhs.uk/live-well/is-my-child-too-ill-for-school/

This webpage offers practical advice for parents if their child has a temperature, has been sick, has a virus or infection, or has more minor ailments such as a sore throat or a cough and cold. Importantly, the NHS said:

> It's normal for children to feel a little anxious sometimes. They may get a tummy ache or headache, or have problems eating or sleeping. Avoiding school can make a child's anxiety about going to school worse. It's good to talk about any worries they may have such as bullying, friendship problems, schoolwork or sensory problems. You can also work with the school to find ways to help them. If your child is still struggling and it's affecting their everyday life, it might be good to talk to your GP or school nurse.

2. **The Children's Commissioner's guide for parents to working together to improve attendance, which can be found at** *https://assets.childrenscommissioner. gov.uk/wpuploads/2022/12/aaa-guide-for-parents-on-school-attendance.pdf*

This online guide says

> being in school and having the best attendance possible underpins all the many benefits of school for your child, such as their learning, wellbeing and wider development. For

some children, attending school every day will be harder than for others. This is why schools, and local councils in some cases, are committed to working together with families to solve problems and support your child's school attendance.

The guide covers two areas:

- Parents' responsibilities for school attendance and what they need to do when their child needs to be absent

- How schools and local authorities will work with parents to support their child's attendance

Under 'parents' responsibilities', the guide makes clear that "as a parent, you are legally responsible for making sure your child gets a suitable full-time education", and "whilst some absence is unavoidable, it is important that your child is in school every day they can be for their learning, wellbeing and development".

The guide says that if a child needs to be absent from school, parents should contact their school as early as possible on the first day of absence to explain why.

The guide also offers some helpful advice to parents about what to do if their child needs support with their attendance. The advice is useful for schools, too.

In the event a learner is absenting themselves due to issues at school, the guide says that parents

should still do everything you can to help your child attend as much as possible whilst waiting for help and support to be put into place. . . . If your child is struggling to attend because of something that is happening at school, their school is expected to work with you (and your child if they are old enough) to overcome the issues. You should agree a set of joint actions with the school that you have all developed together to support your child. This will often include a commitment to support you and your child by working together or help you to access support services in exchange for an agreement from you (and your child if they are old enough to understand) to take part in the support offered. The school will also arrange times for you to come together to review these actions and your child's progress. Depending on the reasons for your child's absence, this may take the form of an action plan, an early help plan, or a parenting contract.

In the event a learner is struggling to attend because of an issue at home, the guide says that the school is expected to help parents access the support they need – such as from a school nurse or local housing or transport team.

Your local council's school attendance team is expected to work with the school and provide access to the support you need if the issues you or your child are facing are beyond the remit of the school. If there are lots of reasons for your child's absence, local services are expected to work together to support you and your child. They are expected to provide you with a single action plan and lead worker to help and support you. In most cases this will be a member of school staff but it might be a member of local council or local healthcare staff. In exchange, you are expected to agree and take part in accessing the support once it has been put in place. It is advisable to regularly meet with your child's school to review what is and isn't working, involving your child if possible. While waiting for help, you should still do everything you can to help your child attend as much as possible.

If a child has a long-term illness or special educational needs and disabilities, they have the same right to a suitable full-time education as any other child. To ensure they receive this, the guide says that parents "should work with your child's school to discuss the reasons and make sure the right support is in place. All schools are expected to provide support in these cases".
Schools are expected to do the following:

- Work with parents to make reasonable adjustments to help a learner attend school. These could include adjustments to uniforms, transport, routines, access to support, or lunchtime arrangements.

- Ensure a learner receives the right pastoral care and, in certain cases, consider a time-limited phased return to school where appropriate.

- Work jointly with other services, including the local council and health services.

And finally, in the event of a learner being too anxious to go to school, the guide reminds parents that attending school usually helps to protect a child's mental health, and being anxious or worried about going to school, particularly around the start of the new year or joining a new school or class, is a normal emotion, and not necessarily indicative of an underlying mental health condition. However, if their anxiety continues and becomes an attendance issue, parents "should speak to your child's school together with your child about why they are anxious and what can be done".

A school's legal duties

So far, we have explored a parent's legal obligations. What, then, must schools do to uphold their legal duties on attendance?
To manage and improve attendance effectively, all schools are expected to:

- Develop and maintain a whole school culture that promotes the benefits of high attendance.

- Have a clear school attendance policy which all staff, learners, and parents understand.

- Accurately complete admission and, with the exception of schools where all learners are boarders, attendance registers and have effective day-to-day processes in place to follow-up absence.

- Regularly monitor and analyse attendance and absence data to identify learners or cohorts that require support with their attendance and put effective strategies in place.

- Build strong relationships with families, listen to and understand barriers to attendance, and work with families to remove them.

40 Why School Doesn't Work for Every Child

- Share information and work collaboratively with other schools in the area, local authorities, and other partners when absence is at risk of becoming persistent or severe.

Which brings us back to the first P in our 5P framework: policy.

As a minimum, a school's attendance policy should detail:

- The attendance and punctuality expectations of learners and parents, including start and close of the day, register closing times, and the processes for requesting leaves of absence and informing the school of the reason for an unexpected absence.

- The name and contact details of the senior leader responsible for the strategic approach to attendance in school.

- Information and contact details of the school staff who learners and parents should contact about attendance on a day-to-day basis (such as a form tutor, attendance officer etc.) and for more detailed support on attendance (such as a head of year, pastoral lead, family liaison officer, etc.).

- The school's day-to-day processes for managing attendance, for example, first-day calling and processes to follow up on unexplained absences.

- How the school is promoting and incentivising good attendance.

- The school's strategy for using data to target attendance improvement efforts to the learners or learner cohorts who need it most.

- The school's strategy for reducing persistent and severe absence, including determining how access to wider support services will be provided to remove the barriers to attendance and when support will be formalised in conjunction with the local authority.

- The point at which Fixed Penalty Notices for absence and other sanctions will be sought if support is not appropriate (e.g., for an unauthorised holiday in term time), not successful, or not engaged with.

Putting the policy into practice

Improving school attendance begins at the board level; therefore, all academy trust boards and governing bodies of maintained schools should take an active role in attendance improvement, support their school to prioritise attendance and work together with school leaders to set whole school attendance cultures.

This should include:

- Setting high expectations of all leaders, staff, learners, and parents.

- Recognising that attendance improvement does not happen in isolation and therefore ensuring it is prioritised in wider improvement strategies, such as raising attainment, behaviour, special educational needs and disabilities, wellbeing, and safeguarding. This may include having a link governor or trustee that focusses on attendance.

- Ensuring the schools' attendance management processes are delivered effectively and that consistent attendance support is provided for learners who require it most by prioritising the staff and resources needed. This includes ensuring schools engage and work effectively with the local authority School Attendance Support Team and wider local partners and services.

- Ensuring high aspirations are maintained for all learners, but that processes and support are adapted to the individual needs of particular learners. This includes those with long-term illnesses, special educational needs, and disabilities, learners with a social worker, and learners from cohorts with historically lower attendance, such as those eligible for free school meals.

- Repeatedly evaluating the effectiveness of their school's processes and improvement efforts to ensure they are meeting the needs of learners as experiences and barriers to attendance evolve.

The key components of an attendance policy should include the following:

- The principles underlying the policy and how they apply to the whole school community:
  - How the policy ties into the school's approach to promoting emotional well-being
  - How the policy links with the school's other policies
  - How these principles relate to the school's overall aims and relate to the rest of the curriculum

- The policy's aims and targets:
  - Specific but realistic targets for improving and maintaining attendance figures
  - The resources a school invests in improving attendance

- The rights, roles, and responsibilities of governors, staff, learners, and parents:
  - The school's partnership agreement with the Education Welfare Service
  - The legal responsibilities of the LA, school, and parents
  - Emphasis on a partnership approach between senior leaders, governors, and those working to support attendance with parents and learners

- The procedures related to the policy:
  - The stages, processes, and staffing involved in registration
  - The system for lateness
  - How and when problems with attendance are communicated to parents
  - Processes used to reintegrate students returning to school after an absence
  - Referral criteria to support services

42 Why School Doesn't Work for Every Child

- The attendance strategies routinely used by the school:
  - How rewards and sanctions are used to encourage regular attendance
  - The methods and means of achieving the school's strategies, including any training required for staff involved in implementation

- Arrangements for monitoring and evaluation:
  - How the school will evaluate the effectiveness of its strategies
  - When monitoring and evaluation will take place
  - Who will be involved in monitoring and evaluation, and how they will contribute
  - How evaluations will be fed back into policy.

Here are some key questions to consider when rewriting your attendance policy:

- How will you seek the views of children to inform your approach to promoting good attendance?
- How will your ethos and goals inform your approach to promoting good attendance?
- How will you communicate your policies to everyone involved with the school, including parents, and ensure they contribute and take ownership?
- How will you make sure your policy links to other pertinent statutory policies, including safeguarding, behaviour, and bullying?
- Who will be accountable and responsible for what?
- How will you set clear and high standards using positive language? How will you use rewards and sanctions?
- What support and training will you provide for all staff, including non-teaching staff and governors?
- What support will you provide for parents and carers who want to learn more about how to help their children do well?
- How will you monitor and evaluate your policies and consult on reviewing them so that they are fair and applied consistently?

Communicating the policy

As I have said, a policy is of no use if that's all it remains. Its contents must be known and understood by all your stakeholders if it is to make a difference. But this is not just about sharing the policy *after* it is written; it's about involving your stakeholders in the process of writing or reviewing the policy. This talks to a school leadership mantra I've long repeated: consultation, *then* communication.

First, consult on your new or revised policy with as many people as possible, asking for contributions from staff, governors, learners, parents, and members of the community, local employers, the local authority, and so on, and ask them about the content, structure, and style of your policy. Ask: does it say what needs to be said, is it simple to navigate, is it easy to understand, does it make sense? and so on.

Second, share your policy with as many people as possible, as often as possible, and in as many different forms as possible.

Talking of forms, think about how accessible your policy is to staff, learners, and parents – both in the sense of how easy it is to find and how easy it is to understand.

Your attendance policy should be on your school's website, but I'd suggest making it one click from your homepage – along with your SEND policy, Pupil Premium Strategy, behaviour policy, and safeguarding policy. And then, I'd suggest doing something different: rather than having your policy uploaded to your website as a PDF, break it up. Your policy is likely to have several headings and subheadings – it will, by necessity, be lengthy. So why not convert your policy's contents page into a set of hyperlinks so that your stakeholders can click on the section they need and be taken to a shorter block of text? Each hyperlink could be connected to a separate page or take visitors to the relevant part of the page they're on.

Next, try to reduce the amount of text and make that text as simple as possible to read. Use monosyllabic words and simple sentences. Avoid figurative language or unfamiliar turns of phrase. Ask those for whom English is an additional language to comment on the draft policy. Is any of it unclear, ambiguous, or hard to decode? Make a version available in brail and in the dominant languages spoken by members of your community.

Also, try to dual-code your policy to reduce the amount of text required. Add icons and diagrams, flow charts, and process maps to help readers navigate the text and understand it. Certainly, process maps are useful ways of articulating what parents are expected to do and when including reporting an unexpected absence or requesting a leave of absence. Or go further: as well as having a written policy, produce short explainer videos on the key messages contained within it, such as why attendance matters and what to do if you think your child is too ill for school. These videos, which could make use of moving graphics and music, could be shared through your website and via emails, text messages, and social media.

Whatever you do, make sure you communicate your policy many times in many different ways. Think about the learner journey: what information would be most useful at various points of the year? What's the best means of communicating that information in a way that has traction and that nudges parents to respond to a call to action?

5 Attendance personalisation and practice

2 Personalisation

The second P in my 5P framework is personalisation because, having said that consistency is key, that is not to suggest that every learner is the same and should be treated the same. Of course, different learners have different needs and face different challenges in attending school and being on time.

To this end, and whilst continuing to work within the confines of the policy, it is important to identify the barriers that individual learners face. For each learner who misses school or is late to school, you should ask yourself, 'Why?' What has prevented this child from attending? Is it something at home or in school? Only by truly analysing the causes can we begin to find workable solutions.

Once the causes of non-attendance are known, the next step is to plan personalised strategies to help support the learner back into school. Here, it is crucial that attempts are made to involve – and not just inform – parents, families, and external agencies in the process.

Without parental support and understanding, it is unlikely that any strategies will be effective in the long term. A learner needs to see that the school and home are united in a common cause, working together and talking to each other.

Once the strategies have been agreed, it is important to set success criteria. Everyone needs to know what a good outcome will look like, how this is going to be achieved, and within what timescales. It may be that step goals are established to encourage a gradual improvement over time, accepting that perfect attendance is an unlikely immediate outcome.

Whilst every learner has a right to a full-time education and high attendance expectations should be set for all learners, an effective attendance policy accounts for the specific needs of certain learners and cohorts.

A policy should be applied fairly and consistently, but in doing so, schools should always consider the individual needs of learners and their families who have specific barriers to attendance.

Schools should also consider their obligations under the Equality Act 2010 and the UN Convention on the Rights of the Child. This involves understanding the possible causes of absence. Here are some possible factors to consider:

Family factors:

- Parents not being aware of attendance law and their obligations
- Parents/carers not understanding or respecting the value of education
- Parents not actively monitoring – or seeming to care about – their child's whereabouts
- A lack of parental insistence that their child should go to school in the morning
- Parents working multiple jobs
- Single parent families
- Competing family priorities: for example, conflicts, getting organised, babysitting, interpreting for non-English speaking parents, transport issues, holidays, or learners expected to care for other family members

Socio-economic factors:

- A lack of affordable transportation to school
- Parents/carers' employment obligations; inflexible employers
- The need for the child to work in order to supplement family incomes
- Domestic violence, child abuse or neglect, drug or alcohol abuse
- High family mobility rates; transient lifestyles
- A lack of affordable childcare for learners with parenting responsibilities
- Cultural obligations: for example, commitments by families to attend significant cultural events

Learner factors:

- Negative experiences at school in the past
- A lack of interest in school and the purpose of education
- Low levels of knowledge about future pathways and the links between school attendance, educational outcomes, and success in work
- Low levels of attention in lessons
- Low levels of literacy and/or numeracy creating a barrier to learning
- A general dislike of the school environment
- Social competence and confidence, leading to conflict or isolation
- Being bullied, feeling unsafe, or having anxiety

- Learners' health and wellbeing; for example, low self-esteem, high levels of anxiety or physical health
- Drug and alcohol use
- A need to demonstrate 'adult' behaviour, a rejection of authority
- Difficulties at the time of transitions

Next, we need to follow a cycle as follows:

Figure 5.1 Assess, plan, do, review cycle

Assess

The assess stage involves gathering information about why a learner has been absent and about the level of engagement we can expect from their families. In practice, we should try to gather information about:

- The reasons and underlying causes of absences
- Patterns and trends of absence
- School-based barriers to attendance
- Home-based barriers to attendance
- Learner-based barriers to attendance
- Anticipated levels of parental engagement

We should gather as much information as we can from:

- Parents and families
- The learner
- School staff

Attendance personalisation and practice **47**

- The local authority
- External agencies

Plan

The second stage is 'plan'. This involves direct work with learners and their parents and families to set out expectations and agree on targets and actions. Action plans should be written in partnership with the learner and their parents, as well as with the local authority and external agencies where appropriate. These plans should then be shared with all parties and reviewed within appropriate timescales.

Do

In the 'do' stage, we work on attendance improvement efforts, removing barriers, and supporting the learner and their parents. We should advise parents as soon as possible when an action plan is not working or working as effectively as we had hoped, and we should set out the reasons for this and its implications. It might be that the plan needs revisiting and actions and timescales changing, or it might mean we have to escalate concerns, moving from voluntary towards more formal support.

The 'do' stage is about removing barriers to attendance, putting in place attendance interventions, and working directly with the learner and their families, including by making home visits where relevant. It might also involve reintegration support, the engagement of multi-agency support, and alternative provision.

Review

In the 'review' stage, all parties need to consider the impact of their actions on improving levels of attendance. We also need to review what worked and what did not and why. We want to assess what we can take away as institutional intelligence to help us improve as a school, speeding up subsequent improvement efforts. And we need to assess next steps. What do we need to do next in order to maintain or further improve the learner's attendance?

3 Practice

The third P in my 5P framework is practice because, once the policy has been agreed and communicated, and the causes and solutions to non-attendance have been targeted and personalised, we must approach the management of attendance and punctuality with high expectations.

One way to exhibit high expectations is to promote a greater awareness – among learners and their parents and families – that an absence results in quantifiable lost learning time. As such, we should try to talk about absence in terms that learners and parents will easily understand – for example, 'missing a day a week means missing out on two weeks of lessons each term'.

48 Why School Doesn't Work for Every Child

Another way to promote high expectations is to inform parents and families about the current research that links good attendance not only with academic achievement but with longer-term health and well-being, not to mention improved job prospects and earning potential. This evidence should, where possible, be localised. Better still, we should find case studies from our own school to prove the research true.

High expectations are also upheld by working in partnership with parents and families to ensure they do not condone absences for trivial reasons and know that family holidays should be taken during the school holidays, not during term time. One way to convince parents of the importance of doing this is to explain that teachers plan sequential lessons and that, as such, absences can severely disrupt learners' progress. It is very difficult to catch up on lessons lost and impossible to recapture the experience of quality first teaching through homework or even one-to-one intervention.

High expectations should also mean taking a rigorous approach to unexplained absences and always following up with parents who have not provided an explanation for their child's absence.

If attendance is to be managed effectively, staff also need to be appropriately skilled – including in how to hold sensitive conversations with learners and their parents. This may involve training and/or coaching, and it will certainly require high levels of support from school leaders.

Alongside accurate recording of attendance and punctuality, schools need robust day-to-day processes to track and follow up on absences and lateness, which are rigorously applied across the school. As a minimum, schools should put in place processes to:

- Define lateness, including in their attendance policy. When does present become late, and when does late become absent? What is the length of time the register will be open, after which a learner will be marked as absent? Whatever definition the school settles on, it should be the same for every lesson, and depending on the structure of the school day, not longer than either 30 minutes after the lesson begins or the length of the form time or first lesson in which the statutory morning registration takes place.

- Ensure that parents contact the school when their child is absent to explain the reason and, if contact is not made within a set timeframe, contact parents to ascertain the reason for absence and when the learner is likely to return. If absence continues without explanation, further contact should be made to ensure safeguarding, and this, ideally, should involve a home visit.

- Input the register code when the reason for an absence is not known at the time the register is taken but subsequently becomes known whilst retaining the evidence trail.

- Regularly inform parents about their child's attendance and do so in a meaningful way, avoiding headline percentages. For example, notify parents of the amount of time missed and the likely impact on their child's learning.

- Meet with the parents of learners who the school considers to be vulnerable or are persistently or severely absent to discuss attendance improvement strategies and their re-engagement in school. Identify learners who need support from wider partners as quickly as possible and make the necessary referrals.

Attendance personalisation and practice **49**

- Support learners back into school following a lengthy or unavoidable period of absence and ensure any attendance improvement strategies – such as part-time timetables – are complemented with pastoral interventions to rebuild the learner's confidence and social and emotional skills.

As we've seen, disadvantaged learners and learners with other risk factors, such as SEND, face greater barriers to attendance than their peers. But their right to an education is the same as any other learner, and, therefore, our expectations of attendance should be the same. That said, we need to be mindful of the additional barriers these learners face and put in place appropriate, additional support where necessary. The provision of additional support should always be made in partnership with parents. This support might include:

- Making reasonable adjustments where a learner has a disability or putting in place an individual healthcare plan where necessary

- Working with parents to ensure the provision outlined in a learner's education, health, and care plan (EHCP) is honoured

- Working with families to help support healthy morning routines and to ensure the learner has access to transportation and the equipment needed in school. Where necessary, make reasonable adjustments to the school's uniform policy, social norms and routines, homework, lunchtime arrangements, and so on

Part-time timetables

If we were to take a significant amount of time off work for illness, we might expect to be offered a staggered return to work, perhaps reducing our daily hours or working fewer days a week. And yet, we rarely extend this privilege to learners.

It's true that, as I said earlier, the law entitles all learners of compulsory school age to a full-time education. However, in exceptional circumstances where it is deemed to be in a learner's long-term interests, schools can agree to operate a part-time timetable. For example, where a medical condition prevents a learner from attending full-time education and a part-time timetable is considered as part of a reintegration package, then this strategy should not be swerved.

There are some important caveats to note, though:

Firstly, a part-time timetable should not be used to manage a learner's behaviour; it is there only to help a learner return to school following a lengthy absence.

Secondly, a part-time timetable should be temporary – indeed, it should be as short-term as possible. When it is agreed upon, a deadline for it to end and review dates should be agreed upon, too.

Thirdly, a part-time timetable should not be regarded as the solution to a learner's attendance issues. Rather, it should be used as a part of a package of reintegration strategies. In most cases, the part-time timetable should run alongside a programme of pastoral support.

50 Why School Doesn't Work for Every Child

Finally, in agreeing to a part-time timetable, a school is agreeing to a learner being absent for part of the week or day and must therefore treat absence as authorised.

Staff training

One of my mantras for improving attendance was 'it's everyone's business'. Every member of staff working in a school has a responsibility to ensure learners attend and do so on time, not least because non-attendance and lateness can be a safeguarding risk. But, in order for all staff to perform their duties, they need to be appropriately knowledgeable and skilled and supported from the top.

As such, attendance should feature as part of a school's planned programme of professional development.

I'd suggest that all staff in school, not just teachers, have annual training on attendance, ideally at the start of the school year. This training should cover the following:

- The contents of the school attendance policy

- The processes your school follows in respect of leaves of absence

- The processes your school follows in respect of unexpected absences

- The processes your school follows in respect of lateness

- How to have sensitive conversations with learners about attendance and punctuality

- The underlying causes of non-attendance and lateness

On the last point, I would suggest you return to what I said earlier about the factors affecting attendance, including:

- Mental health and anxiety

- Poverty and the cost of living

- Housing and transportation

- SEND and other risk factors

- Changes in family circumstances

- Fear of minor illness/misunderstanding of reasons for absence

All staff need annual training because, just as the barriers to attendance are constantly evolving, so too is the advice that staff need to address them.

In addition to training, the previous information should also form part of new staff's induction, and there should be opportunities for staff taking up a post in-year to access the same information.

All staff training should promote the importance of good attendance and make clear that absence is almost always a symptom of wider circumstances. It should cover a school's legal requirements, including the keeping of registers, monitoring, tracking, evaluating, and following up on absences, and the strategies deployed to improve attendance. It should also set out the school's processes for working with other partners to provide more intensive support to those learners who need it. Training should also equip all staff with up-to-date knowledge of the latest government guidance and regulations.

Those colleagues with particular responsibilities around attendance, such as form tutors and pastoral staff, need tailored training on top of the all-staff training mentioned previously, including:

- Taking registers accurately and on time

- The correct use of attendance codes

- Identifying and reporting safeguarding concerns

- Working with families to remove barriers to attendance

Further, those staff with responsibility for data analysis and reporting need training on:

- How to monitor attendance data to identify learners at risk

- How to evaluate attendance data to identify patterns and trends

- How to extrapolate data for individual learners, groups of learners, and cohorts of learners

- How to report attendance data to stakeholders, including governors

We'll return to the subject of data analysis later.

Intervention strategies

In terms of knowing what attendance improvement strategies work in practice, it's important for schools to utilise two sources of evidence: external evidence and internal evidence.

External evidence is that which is available from outside the school, including in the form of meta-analyses and randomised control trials, as well as information shared by the government and organisations such as the Education Endowment Foundation (EEF).

The EEF has conducted some research into attendance interventions. They have analysed the impact of:

- Mentoring

- Parental engagement

- Responsive and targeted approaches

- Teaching of social and emotional skills

- Behaviour interventions

- Meal provision

- Incentives and disincentives

- Extra-curricular activities

Their findings are not yet conclusive, but early indications suggest that two of the previously mentioned interventions are particularly effective. Those interventions are parental engagement and responsive and targeted approaches.

Internal evidence is that which is gathered within your school. I'd suggest that schools should become rich in institutional intelligence by analysing what works and what doesn't within their setting. Every intervention should be monitored and evaluated so that they can be improved for the learner being supported and so that the school can carry forward information that will make their subsequent attendance improvement work more efficient and impactful.

Internal evidence is not just the results of intervention strategies but also an ongoing analysis of attendance data in order to identify patterns and trends and thus become proactive and data-driven. I'll explore this later when we look at performance data.

In terms of interventions, it might be helpful to think in terms of a hierarchy.

First, there are those interventions which all learners have access to and which benefit all learners. These interventions tend to be preventative. They include:

- The use of clear, concise, and consistent communication with learners and parents

- The promotion of high expectations around attendance and punctuality

- The establishment of habits and routines related to attendance

- Personalised positive communications with parents when learners are absent

- The recognition and celebration of good and/or improving attendance

- The availability of a named member of staff for every learner to turn to

Second, there are those interventions which are used when a learner first shows signs of being absent. These interventions tend to be corrective. They include:

- The identification of common barriers to attendance

- The removal of school-based barriers

- Parental engagement, including home visits to help remove home-based barriers

- The use of specialist support services to help remove learner-based barriers

- The co-construction with parents of an individual attendance improvement plan

- The use of mentors, including peer mentors or small group interventions

Third, there are those interventions which are used when a learner's absence has become persistent or severe. These interventions tend to be more intensive or formal. They include:

- The formal use of attendance improvement plans

- The engagement of multi-agency support

- Statutory intervention (as a last resort)

Celebrations over sanctions

In line with my earlier advice to promote the benefits of good attendance and to flip the conversation to avoid a deficit model, I'd suggest we focus on celebrating good attendance more than we attempt to punish learners for poor attendance.

But here's an important caveat: there is a difference between incentivising attendance and rewarding it.

Rewards such as certificates and prizes for 100% attendance are, though well-intentioned, problematic. As we have seen, not all learners are equal, and many learners face additional barriers to attendance than their peers. Rewarding 100% attendance indirectly discriminates against some learners, including those with a protected characteristic – such as a disability – under the Equality Act 2010. Rather than focus on headline attendance statistics, I'd suggest we reward *improved* attendance. Or, rather than reward attendance at all, we incentivise it . . .

Incentives are motivations to encourage learners to attend. Incentives focus on the journey, not the destination, on the promotion of good attendance, and not on the level of attendance achieved. As such, incentives can level the playing field for all learners.

Here are some tips for making a success of attendance incentives:

1. Think through the changes you're trying to cultivate and ensure your incentives are designed to achieve this.

2. Consider incentives for shorter periods of time so that all learners and parents can be successful.

3. Include learners and parents in the consultation when deciding what to incentivise and how.

4. Recognise parents and families, not just learners, when attendance improvement efforts work.

5. Offer incentives that will help to address any barriers to attendance, such as school equipment, uniform items, alarm clocks, food hampers, etc.

Returning to Public First, whose report I shared earlier, the think tank offered the following recommendations for putting attendance improvement efforts into practice:

Firstly, they suggest providing "intensive, nuanced support to families for whom attendance is a significant issue". They say that "engaging 'parents as partners' is crucial in tackling attendance; how, when and by whom parents are spoken to matters hugely".

Secondly, they suggest "better joined up working and signposting to the appropriate agencies would ensure that those best placed to offer support were doing so". Further, they argue that a clearer understanding of which agencies could and should address wider issues that families are experiencing would also "reduce 'school blaming' whereby parents hold schools accountable for all problems in their lives".

Thirdly, they suggest improving the accuracy of school-level attendance monitoring systems so that "information shared with parents is accurate [which would] boost confidence from parents that the information they are being given about their child is accurate". Furthermore, "reducing incorrect information would improve school-parent relationships and allow schools to better target their support".

Supporting learners with mental health issues

As I've said, some learners face greater barriers to attendance than others, and schools need to make reasonable adjustments to avoid indirectly discriminating against some learners on the basis of their additional need. When it comes to supporting the attendance of learners with mental health issues, I'd suggest the following approach:

A. Prevent mental health issues

- Create a safe and calm environment which promotes good health and wellbeing, including good mental health.

- Explicitly teach learners about mental health and equip them with strategies – such as mindfulness – for dealing with mental health problems, including anxiety.

- Help learners to develop resilience and self-regulation by modelling it and by sharing practical strategies such as self-assessment.

B. Identify mental health issues

- Train staff to recognise emerging issues as early and accurately as possible and ensure there is a robust reporting system in place to refer learners for support.

- Help learners to access evidence-informed early support and interventions.

- Work effectively with external agencies to provide timely access to specialist support.

C. Develop whole-school approaches

- Develop an effective whole-school approach which champions efforts to promote mental health and wellbeing.

- Appoint a governor with knowledge and understanding of mental health and wellbeing issues and ensure mental health is discussed at governing body meetings.

- Appoint a senior leader responsible for mental health who can provide the strategic leadership needed to successfully implement the whole school approach to mental health and wellbeing.

- Ensure mental health and wellbeing are referenced in the school improvement plan and in school policies so that actions are integrated, sustained, and monitored for impact.

D. Involve learners and parents

- Involve learners and parents in developing mental health plans and policies so that they are responsive to the evolving needs of the school community.

- Gather ongoing feedback from all stakeholders – including staff – to promote mental health and wellbeing across the school.

- Parents and families play a key role in supporting their child's mental health and wellbeing. Therefore, we should ensure that the mental health and wellbeing support offer is clearly communicated with parents and work closely with the local authority to ensure parents are aware of the wider support available to them.

E. Establish the ethos and environment

- Attend to the physical, social, and emotional environment so that the school promotes an ethos of respect and tolerance and creates a safe environment for those who have experienced trauma and adverse experiences.

- Foster healthy relationships between staff and learners that help engender a sense of belonging to and liking of the school.

F. Create the curriculum

- Plan for the teaching of social and emotional skills that will improve academic progress and benefit health and wellbeing, including though not exclusively through the Personal, Social, Health, and Economic Education (PSHE) curriculum. Make sure learners are able to recognise what is normal and what is an issue in themselves and others, and when issues arise, know how to seek support as early as possible from appropriate sources. Further, make sure learners understand how they are feeling and why, develop the language that they use to talk about their bodies, health, and emotions, and understand where normal variations in emotions end and health and wellbeing issues begin.

- Identify points in the academic year where there are natural opportunities for a specific focus on mental health, such as teaching the skills needed for coping with periods of transition and change and the skills needed for handling the pressures of exams.

G. Support staff health and wellbeing

- It's not just about learners; schools also need to promote good staff health and wellbeing. Provide opportunities for staff to reflect on and take actions to enhance their own wellbeing and promote a healthy work-life balance. Signpost sources of help and advice include the charity Education Support which is dedicated to improving the health and wellbeing of the education workforce. The Better Health Every Mind Matters website also includes a self-care tool to help staff take simple steps to look after their mental health and find a good work-life balance.

Attendance performance data and parents

4 Performance data

The fourth P in my 5P framework is performance data because a school needs an effective electronic system that provides effective data in a timely manner. Here, it is important that data is monitored 'live', so to speak, as well as evaluated later, such as at the end of a week, month, term, or year. If data is monitored contemporaneously, then action can be taken quickly. The subsequent data analysis should include trends over time (although attendance might still be lower than desired, it may be improving), as well as patterns for different groups of learners (such as by gender, ethnicity, learning needs, etc.) and cohorts of learners (such as by year group, key stage, subject, etc.). Patterns can also emerge across the school week, term, and year.

Having effective data enables schools to move towards a data-driven attendance improvement strategy, which allows the early identification of learners at risk of poor attendance. It's the difference between being proactive – predicting attendance pinch-points and problems and acting to prevent them – and reactive – responding after learners have become absent.

To ensure that attendance data is valid and reliable, and therefore useful and useable, it may be necessary to train staff on inputting attendance marks and on monitoring and evaluating the data – making sure the system inputs and outputs can be trusted. It may also be necessary to regularly reiterate to staff the importance of filing accurate and prompt registers, as well as the appropriate use of codes and discerning lateness from absence in a consistent manner.

Once attendance data has been analysed, it needs to be acted upon and this means providing intervention and support. As I've already said, it's crucial that schools intervene early if a learner's attendance begins to deteriorate, and this includes offering support to parents if their child refuses to go to school.

Intervention may involve addressing school-based barriers to attendance, such as bullying and friendship issues. It might involve providing uniforms, stationery, and/or textbooks to learners in financial need and whose lack of resources causes embarrassment from which they want to absent themselves. Intervention may also involve setting up a learner support group which explores the reasons for absences and develops an attendance improvement plan or a 'return to school' plan. Intervention may take the form of specialist support from external agencies such as health professionals or enlisting the help and advice of other schools, organisations, and community groups. And finally, intervention may be about enlisting a mentor for those learners who are at risk.

Back to data . . . the law requires all schools in England to have an admission register and an attendance register. All learners (regardless of their age) must be placed on the admission register and have their attendance recorded in the attendance register. To fail to do this is an offence – and that's a point worth sharing with staff to underline the importance of everyone taking responsibility for attendance.

Schools must take the attendance register at the start of each morning session of each school day and once during each afternoon session. On each occasion, they must record whether every learner is "present, attending an approved educational activity, absent, or unable to attend due to exceptional circumstances".

Another point worth sharing with staff is that attendance registers are legal records, and all schools must preserve every entry in the attendance register for three years from the date of entry. The government guidance says that "as the attendance register is a record of the learners present at the time it was taken, the register should only routinely be amended where the reason for absence cannot be established at the time it is taken and it is subsequently necessary to correct the entry. Where amendments are made, all schools must ensure the register shows the original entry, the amended entry, the reason for the amendment, the date on which the amendment was made, and the name and title of the person who made the amendment".

Effective data analysis involves identifying and then providing support to learners, groups of learners, and cohorts of learners whose attendance is or is at risk of becoming a concern. In practice, this involves:

- Monitoring daily attendance and following up on any unexplained absences as soon as possible.

- Analysing weekly attendance to identify patterns and trends so that we can deliver appropriate and timely interventions in a targeted way to learners and their families.

- Providing regular attendance reports to teachers to help them have discussions with learners.

- Providing regular attendance reports to school leaders, including the SENDCo, Designated Safeguarding Lead, and Pupil Premium Coordinator, to help them plan strategic responses and identify learners at risk.

- Providing regular attendance reports to the governing body to help them support and challenge the school's attendance improvement efforts.

- Analysing half-termly, termly, and full-year data to identify patterns and trends, including in the use of attendance codes, days of poor attendance, and, where appropriate, subjects which have low lesson attendance.

- Benchmarking attendance data against local, regional, and national levels to identify areas of focus for improvement.

- Evaluating the impact of attendance improvement efforts, including any interventions, and using the findings to help inform future strategies.

- Ensuring governors regularly review attendance data at board meetings, including a thorough examination of recent and historical trends at a school level as well as benchmarking to comparator schools, then working with school leaders to set goals or areas of focus for attendance and providing support and challenge around delivery against those focus areas.

5 Parents

The fifth and final P in my 5P framework is parents, but it's fair to say that parents and families run right through my framework like a golden thread. Put simply, without parental support, we cannot secure good attendance and punctuality.

I will explore the importance of parental engagement in more depth in Chapter 12 and consider some practical ways of ensuring parents become partners in their child's education. Here, I'll focus solely on the role parents can play in helping improve attendance.

It is important that parents and families are not only informed about matters relating to attendance but are also fully involved in the process. Parents should be regarded as partners in the process of securing good attendance – that way, they will better understand the importance of attendance and punctuality, be more able and willing to uphold high expectations at home, and accept any sanctions or referrals to outside agencies.

One way to help parents become partners is to use technology to alert parents to non-attendance as soon as it comes to light. For example, text messages and emails are more effective at flagging issues as they happen rather than trying to make phone contact or send letters after the event.

Not only is it helpful to consult with parents on the contents of an attendance policy, as I said earlier, but it's also wise to collaborate with parents on their child's attendance improvement plan or 'return to school' plan. Often, these plans address practical issues such as getting an alarm clock, negotiating transport, or changing family routines – and parents are better placed than teachers to ensure these things happen.

A partnership is a two-way process, of course, and so the school should encourage parents to seek support from and communicate regularly with, school leaders and teachers when help or advice is needed.

Schools should treat all learners and parents with dignity and respect, and staff should model respectful relationships to build a positive connection between home and school that can be the foundation of good attendance. In communicating with parents, schools should discuss the link between attendance and attainment and wider wellbeing, and challenge parents' views where they have misconceptions about what 'good' attendance looks like. Where a learner or their family needs support with attendance, it is important that the best-placed person in the school works with and supports the family and, wherever possible, the person should be kept consistent.

Where a pattern of absence is at risk of becoming, or becomes, problematic, the school should draw on these relationships and listen to and understand the barriers to attendance the learner or their family is experiencing. In doing so, schools should take into consideration the sensitivity of some of the reasons for absence and understand the importance of school as a place of safety and support rather than reaching out immediately for punitive approaches.

In the first instance, schools should support learners and parents by working together to address any in-school barriers to attendance. Then, where barriers exist outside of school, all partners should work together to support learners and parents to voluntarily access the support they need. As a minimum, this should include meeting with the parents of those learners who are at risk of persistent or severe absence in order to understand the barriers they face to attendance in school and then to agree on actions or interventions to help overcome them. This may include referrals to specialist services and external organisations that can provide support. Any actions or interventions should then be regularly reviewed with learners and their parents.

Where an absence intensifies, so too should the support provided. This might require the school to work with the local authority and other relevant partners. Support at this stage will depend on the barriers to attendance the learner faces. If the barriers are individual to the learner, then interventions might include mentoring, careers advice, an alternative provision such as part-time access to a college vocational programme, personal tuition, and so on. If the barriers are broader, then interventions might include a voluntary early help assessment.

If one of the barriers is a lack of parental engagement in the process itself, then schools might need to facilitate more formal conversations with parents and wider family members, as well as with the learners themselves if they're old enough. Such conversations should set out the potential consequences of persistent and severe absence to the learner and their parents and make clear the potential for recourse to legal interventions. But, more than anything else, these conversations should be an opportunity to listen to and understand the barriers to attendance that the learner and their parents face, and they should be marked by dignity and respect. These conversations should also signpost parents to the help and support available to them, and – as ever, they should be about what the school can do to help rather than a finger-pointing exercise.

Though we hope to avoid it in most cases, sometimes voluntary support is either ineffective or is not engaged with by learners and parents, and we need to move to a more formal footing. When this happens, schools need to work with their local authority. This might take the form of a parenting contract or an education supervision order. It might include a fixed penalty notice, which is likely to change the parents' behaviour. Where there are safeguarding concerns, especially where absence becomes severe, it may be necessary to intensify support through statutory children's social care involvement. In all cases, the school should monitor the impact of any actions and interventions and, in consultation with the learner and their parents, as well as external partners, make reasonable adjustments where necessary. Where interventions are not working, everyone should work together to understand why and to change the approach.

At the heart of a programme of effective parental engagement on attendance is clear and consistent communication. Communications on attendance need to be timely and regular. It is better to talk to parents early about emerging attendance patterns rather than talk about poor attendance after the event or after absenteeism has become habitual. Communications should be personalised, too, both in the sense that they use the learner's name and that they contain accurate data that is specific to that learner, not generic whole-year or whole-school data. That's not to say that a learner's specific data cannot and should not be placed in context by comparing it to the whole-year or whole-school data. As I've already said, attendance data should also be meaningful. Parents are more likely to understand the data if we frame it in terms of the number of lessons missed or in terms of lost learning. If there are patterns, these should also be shared with parents to help them understand why their child is absent at certain points.

Effective parental communication on attendance is also positive and future-focused. In other words, it encourages parents and families to consider all the benefits of school, not just the academic. For example, it articulates the social and emotional benefits of school and the impact regular schooling can have on a child's health and wellbeing.

Effective parental communication on attendance contains a call to action. In other words, it makes clear the purpose of the communication and what parents are expected to do with it. In most cases, this includes citing relevant aspects of the school's attendance policy and the names and contact details of the members of school staff to whom parents should respond or from whom additional help and support is available when needed. Where parental action is needed, the tone of the communication should be supportive and empathetic and make clear what the school can do to help. It should also avoid the blame game, making clear that the school understands that some families face greater difficulties than others, and yet no family is alone in facing challenges with their child's attendance.

I will talk more in Chapter 12 about methods of communication. Suffice it to say that if we want our messages on attendance to be heard, we need to think about the ways in which those messages are transmitted. This means we think about the accessibility of the communication and the mechanisms we use to communicate it. Think about translating key communications into different languages and having braille versions. Think, too, about reducing the cognitive demand by using short, simple words and short, simple sentences, as well as having icons and flowcharts and bullet points rather than long paragraphs. Think, too, about sending communications via phone calls, letters, text messages, email, on social media, in learners' schoolbags, and so on. Try to ascertain from parents their preferred method of communication and try to find out when it's most convenient to make phone calls home.

Here are some other tips for making a success of parental communications on attendance:

Regularly reiterate the policy

I've already talked at length about the importance of the attendance policy and of communicating it to parents and families. A policy articulates the school's culture of high attendance. Since a policy sets out the trigger points for attendance communications, interventions, and support, it should be shared with parents and families regularly. Include elements of the policy in newsletters, start/end of term emails, regular text messages, and at events such as parent consultation evenings.

Personalise the message

Individualised messages to parents and families often have the most impact because they see the communication as relevant or applicable to them.

Make it easy to access

Research suggests that email is the most convenient and accessible means of communicating less urgent messages but that parents prefer letters for communicating more serious or important information.

Copies of all communications should be archived on the school website to ensure parents don't miss out on important messages.

Social media can also be useful for some, but not all, parents.

Send positive text messages

A study with Bristol City Council[1] found that sending text messages to the parents of learners with attendance below 95% increased good attendance rates by four percentage points.

Research also shows that parents prefer to receive text messages that are unique to their children because this helps them to prioritise their responses.

The key to making a success of text messages is to use them to build relationships and form a bond with parents by keeping them informed. For example, if we send text messages to share positive messages and signposts to help and support, then parents are more likely to engage with them.

Here are some examples of text messages that contain positive and meaningful communications:

"[NAME] has missed [NUMBER] lessons this year. Lessons build on what learners already know, and missing today's lesson will make tomorrow's lesson more difficult".

"Being in school every day supports your child's physical, social, and mental wellbeing, as well as helping them academically".

"It's natural to worry about your child's mental health, but rather than keeping them off school, consider telling us about your concerns. That way, we can work together to support your child".

"We know it can be difficult to know whether your child is too ill to attend school, and that's why the NHS has produced clear guidance [LINK]. For example, they say that it's fine to send a child to school with a minor cough or common cold, provided they don't have a temperature. If in doubt, ask us to help".

"School isn't just about learning; it's a supportive environment where your child can socialise and develop the emotional skills needed for life".

Phone calls are more personal

Most parents prefer phone calls for personal conversations about their children. However, it's important to make sure the right person in school makes those calls. If the phone call is of a sensitive nature, the member of staff should know the learner well and ideally already have a relationship with the family, and they should have the skills needed to have what can be a challenging conversation.

Face-to-face is more friendly

Face-to-face meetings with parents are most helpful when schools need to enlist parents' help in taking action to improve attendance. Whether these meetings take place in person or via video call, and in school or in the community, they offer an opportunity to discuss in detail and with frankness what next steps are needed to support the learner.

Note

1 https://www.bi.team/blogs/improving-student-attendance-through-timely-nudges/

PART II
B is for behaviours

7 Behaviour cultures

Behaviours

So far, we've explored the A of my ABC of creating an inclusive school culture: attendance. Now let's turn to the B, which stands for behaviours. Behaviours come next because, once learners are attending school, we need them to be motivated and engaged.

As I explained in Chapter 2, behaviours is two-fold:

First, learners need to be helped to conduct themselves appropriately and to comply with our rules and expectations.

Second, learners need to be helped to develop positive attitudes to learning and a raft of behaviours for learning so that they can access an increasingly challenging curriculum, actively engage with their studies, and make good progress. *Attitudes to learning* include being resilient and determined, having self-esteem and a belief in your ability to get better with hard work and effort, and having a plan for the future, which provides a source of motivation and a sense of purpose. *Behaviours for learning* take many forms but include study skills such as note-taking and independent research, debate and discussion, self- and peer-assessment, and metacognition and self-regulation.

In practice, this requires five elements:

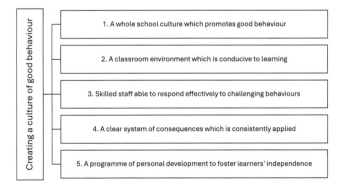

Figure 7.1 Five elements of creating a culture of good behaviour

DOI: 10.4324/9781003520634-10

67

We'll explore all five elements over the course of the next three chapters, starting here with whole-school culture.

1 Whole school culture

As I said in Chapter 2, culture comes from the top. Put simply, a culture is 'the way we do things around here'. Culture is consistency. If every stakeholder involved in a school is to perpetuate their school's culture – to live and breathe their school's values – then they need to know what that culture looks like in practice and why that culture is important to everyone. This involves identifying a set of social norms, habits, and routines which make the culture concrete, then practising those norms until they become automatic for all. It means constantly repeating and reinforcing those norms. And it means making sure every learner can conform to those norms – making reasonable adjustments where necessary.

I have already advocated 'flipping the conversation' around attendance. I have suggested we promote the benefits of good attendance rather than talk in deficit terms about absences. And I apply the same logic here: our inclusive culture should be a positive force for good, it should foster a sense of belonging, it should articulate what every member of the school community has in common and what binds them in a common cause. It should also be future-focused, concentrating on the attributes that learners need in order to be prepared for the next stages of their lives. It should be a source of enrichment, of personal development, not simply a system of sanctions. It should, in short, be about the 'do's', not the 'don'ts', and the 'coulds', not the 'shoulds'.

I think behaviour cultures are best created in three stages by:

Figure 7.2 Creating the culture

1. Creating the culture

Creating the culture is about agreeing on the social norms that you want to see reproduced throughout the school community.

Here, I'd suggest we ask, 'What would I like all learners to do routinely?' 'What do I want them to believe about themselves, their achievements, each other, the school?'

Once these questions have been answered, we can then translate these aspirations into expectations.

2. Communicating the culture

Social norms are found most clearly in the daily routines of the school.

Any aspect of the school culture that can be standardised because it is expected from all learners at all times should be, for example, walking on the left or right of the corridor, entering the class, entering the assembly, and clearing tables at lunch.

These routines should be communicated to and practiced by staff and learners until they become automatic.

This frees up time, mental effort, and energy for more useful areas, such as study.

This means demonstrating it, communicating it thoroughly, and ensuring that every aspect of school life feeds into and reinforces that culture.

3. Continuing the culture

Once built, school systems require regular maintenance – we must not assume that, once it has been created, communicated, and made concrete, our culture will flourish if left alone.

Rather, we need to cultivate that culture continuously. And this requires our constant attention.

Although it is reasonably straightforward to identify what a good culture might look like, much like a diet, the difficulty lies in embedding and maintaining it.

This includes staff training, effective use of consequences, data monitoring, staff and learner surveys, and maintaining standards.

To make the culture continuous, we need to establish the right conditions within which such a culture can flourish, and – amongst other means – this can be done through the use of assemblies, displays, expectations around punctuality and appearance, and what happens if learners do not come to class with the right equipment.

Promoting positive behaviours

When it comes to promoting a culture of positive behaviour, the goal is to provide a calm, safe, and supportive environment which protects learners from disruption and which learners want to attend, and in which they can learn and thrive.

Good behaviour is central to a good education. Where behaviour is poor, learners suffer from lost learning and are more likely to experience anxiety, bullying, and distress. Similarly, the prevalence of poor behaviour negatively affects teachers' health and well-being, and, for some, it is the reason they quit the profession.

Not only is good behaviour important in school, but it is also a door to future success. Being taught how to behave appropriately is a valuable skill that will help learners succeed in their future lives, including in the workplace.

To create the culture in practice, schools need to be clear about which behaviours are permitted and which are prohibited. Further, schools need to set out the values, attitudes, and beliefs they wish to promote as well as the social norms and routines they wish to replicate throughout their school community.

A school's behaviour policy is a crucial starting point for setting out this culture and a means of communicating that culture to learners, staff, parents, and families.

But, as with the attendance policy, a behaviour policy is of little use if it remains a policy; rather, it must be translated into practice, and that means ensuring every member of staff follows the policy for every learner, albeit with pragmatism and humanity.

The best behaviour policies, I think, are founded on a set of shared values, the kinds of attributes we want every learner to adopt and exhibit, and the kinds of behaviours that will help learners to become happy, healthy, and moral people. Those values might include dignity and respect, honesty and integrity, kindness and empathy, trust and diligence, resilience and determination. I could go on. But what's important is that those values are grounded in reality and realised through daily actions. What does it mean to treat people with dignity and respect? What does this look like in tangible terms that learners would understand and be able to emulate? What does it mean to be honest and to act with integrity? Honesty is sometimes difficult, so why is it important? What of kindness, a much-underrated attribute? What might those daily kindnesses look like? And why should we be kind to each other? What's in it for us all? 'Do unto others as you would have them do unto you', the Bible tells us. Kindness begets kindness. The kinder you are to others, the more kindness will be offered to you.

All school staff have a moral – and in some cases, legal – responsibility to provide a safe environment in which learners can thrive, and the school behaviour policy should be written with this in mind; behaviour and safeguarding are two sides of the same coin. Where circumstances arise that endanger the safety of a learner or staff member, the school is duty-bound to act swiftly and decisively to remove the threat and reduce the likelihood of its reoccurrence. The behaviour policy should set out the processes and procedures the school will follow to ensure everyone's safety.

High standards and clear rules should reflect the values of the school and outline the expectations and consequences of behaviour for everyone.

As a minimum, a behaviour policy should include information on the following:

Figure 7.3 Ingredients of a behaviour policy

Purpose: What are the underlying objectives of the policy, what are its aims, and how will it help create a calm, safe, and supportive environment in which all learners can thrive?

People: Who are the key members of staff responsible for behaviour, including senior leaders and governors, and what are their roles?

Process: What are the school systems and social norms underpinning our approach to behaviour? This includes, though it is not limited to, our expectations and rules, the habits and routines we expect to see replicated throughout our school, and the consequences (rewards and sanctions) that will apply when learners do or do not obey our expectations and norms.

Professional development: What support are staff given in their induction and through ongoing training to understand the school policy and to develop a set of skills that enable them to manage behaviour effectively?

Progression: How do we support learners' transitions, including when they transfer schools, so they are inducted and re-inducted into our behaviour systems, rules, and routines?

Pastoral care: What do you do to support learners' social and emotional needs and personal development, including helping those learners with additional needs where those needs might affect their behaviour? What reasonable adjustments do you make to ensure every learner, no matter their additional and different needs, is helped to meet high expectations and engage in school routines?

Protection: What do we do to protect learners from harm, including child-on-child abuse? What do we do to prevent abuse from happening, and how do we respond to incidents of such abuse when they inevitably arise from time to time?

Permitted and prohibited: What do we encourage, and what do we ban?

Further, I'd suggest that our behaviour policy should be underpinned by the following principles:

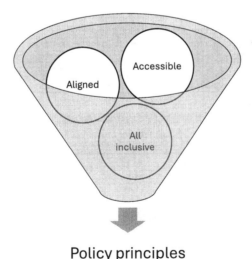

Figure 7.4 Principles of a behaviour policy

Accessible: In the sense that it is easy to gain access to and is easily understood by all stakeholders. Where is the policy kept, and how easily can parents and families find it and find what they're looking for? How accessible is the language used in the policy, and what reasonable adjustments do we make to help those for whom English is an additional language and those with visual impairments to understand it?

Aligned: The behaviour policy should not sit in isolation; it should be linked to other relevant school policies and procedures, including the safeguarding policy, staff development policy, and SEND policy. Do all these policies 'talk to each other' and complement each other? Are the messages they convey coherent?

All inclusive: Your behaviour policy should contain sufficient detail so as to be meaningful and so as to ensure it can be implemented consistently by all staff at all times. The policy also needs to foster a sense of belonging; it needs to be the result of consultation so every member of your school community feels they own it, and understand it, and feel it will do good.

The principles of a behaviour culture

A good behaviour policy provides predictability – both in terms of our expectations and the consequences learners will face if they do not meet those expectations. We would not be too happy if, driving to work tomorrow morning, the police pulled us over and fined us for not wearing a hi-vis jacket whilst at the wheel. The sanction would be heinous because we had not been told in advance about the hi-vis rule. Learners – and their families – need to know what is permitted and what is prohibited, and why, and they need to know what will happen if they do something that is prohibited. It's about transparency; it's about being open and honest. And surely these are values that we want to replicate throughout our school community, too?

Indeed, I would suggest three key values underpin our approach to behaviour: openness, consistency, and fairness.

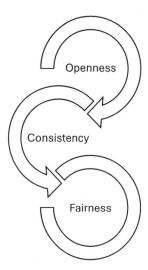

Figure 7.5 Behaviour values

1. Openness

It is important that our rules and routines are known and understood, that every learner in our school knows what is expected of them and understands the consequences they are likely to face should they fail to live up to those expectations.

Ideally, learners should be involved in the process of drawing up the rules or at least be consulted on them once they've been drawn up. It is important that our learners feel your rules are reasonable and appropriate.

Personally, I've always favoured using a learner contract which acts in much the same way as an employment contract: it states what is expected of learners and what they can expect in return from the school. If learners sign it, they feel more like adults; moreover, they feel that they have some ownership of the rules and are, therefore, duty-bound to obey them.

A contract is about giving learners ownership of their behaviour and of the consequences of their actions – showing learners that, with rights come responsibilities – as opposed to telling learners what they can and can't do. Therefore, a contract becomes enabling rather than restricting. The contract, once agreed upon, needs to be articulated to learners and referred to as often as possible.

2. Consistency

Once agreed upon and communicated, it is important that our school rules and routines are (or appear to be) applied consistently: the rules – and the authority and respect of those applying them – will be undermined if one person is punished for an offence while someone else, committing the same offence, escapes punishment or is punished differently.

Often, this is simply about effective communication: explaining what has happened, what action has been taken, and why that action was appropriate (in other words, explain the rationale and explain how a decision is consistent with similar cases), and what will happen next.

3. Fairness

It is important that the school rules are applied fairly and that everyone feels they are treated justly. In practice, this means allowing everyone a right to reply. It is sensible to listen to a range of different opinions before taking action and to involve the 'offender' in the process of agreeing on the consequences of their actions.

Often, a situation arises because a learner feels ignored. They are told off for something they did not do and are not allowed to explain. They grow agitated by this and may become confrontational.

The best thing we can do when trying to resolve the situation is to allow the learner the time and space to calm down and then listen to them; allow the learner to have their say without interruption. This does not mean contradicting the rules or what another teacher or learner has said, nor does it mean being soft. It means being human, being the adult, and being fair.

Once we have listened to the learner's point of view, we can explain how others may perceive the incident and ask the learner to put themselves in other people's shoes for a moment. We should explain that we must also abide by rules, and we, too, would face consequences if we broke them. By getting the learner to see that they are not so different from their teacher, we are again reinforcing the idea of fairness.

The behaviour curriculum

The planned behaviour curriculum

High expectations should pervade all aspects of school life, and this includes not just our behaviour management systems but also how learners are taught to behave appropriately – the behaviour curriculum, if you like.

A behaviour curriculum defines the expected behaviours in school rather than only a list of prohibited behaviours. A behaviour curriculum articulates what good behaviours look like. Whilst a behaviour curriculum does not need to be exhaustive, it does need to represent the key habits and routines required of all learners all the time.

Social norms – daily habits and routines – should promote the values of the school. Any aspect of behaviour that is expected from all learners all the time should be made into an easily and universally understood routine. Social norms might, for example, set out how learners enter and leave the classroom, how learners conduct themselves in the corridors and canteen, such as clearing tables after lunch, and how learners engage in class discussions.

Reasonable adjustments should be made to social norms for those learners who have additional and different needs, including those with protected characteristics under the Equality Act 2010. These adjustments should be proportionate and ensure all learners can meet the school's expectations. Reasonable adjustments are about ensuring equity and fairness, not about lowering expectations or permitting unacceptable behaviours. The adjustments may be temporary or fixed; they may be planned, or they may be proactive.

The hidden behaviour curriculum

Just as there is a planned curriculum and a hidden curriculum, so too are there planned and hidden versions of the behaviour curriculum. The planned behaviour curriculum is what is set out in documents and delivered to learners in a structured way; the hidden behaviour curriculum is what learners are taught in unstructured ways through the behaviour, attitudes, and values exhibited by all the staff who work in the school.

As such, all staff – not just teachers – have an important role to play in not only establishing clear boundaries of acceptable learner behaviour, but in modelling the behaviour they expect to see from others. Staff needs to uphold their school's culture and always obey the policy, and they need to practise expected behaviours and visibly live the school values. This includes positive relationships and always treating others with dignity and respect. It means being honest and acting with integrity. It means being kind and empathetic. Learners need to see – not just be taught about – good habits.

In short, all staff should communicate the school's values and follow the school's agreed social norms in every interaction with colleagues and learners.

Transmitting the behaviour curriculum to learners

All learners are entitled to learn in an environment that is calm, safe, and supportive, and all learners have the right to be treated with dignity. To achieve this, every learner needs to be taught the behaviour curriculum, and this means showing them that with rights come responsibilities that they have a duty to follow the behaviour policy and to uphold the rules and follow the routines.

Parents and families also have a part to play. Parents should be encouraged to get to know the school's behaviour policy because they have an important role in supporting its implementation – something which works best when they reinforce the policy at home as well as in school.

As ever, schools need to build and maintain positive relationships with parents, including by keeping them updated about their child's behaviour, and by encouraging parents to celebrate their child's successes. Where appropriate, parents should also be included in any pastoral work following incidences of misbehaviour.

Behaviour classroom environments

2 Classroom environment

Aristotle once said that "excellence is not an act but a habit", and so it is with teaching: the foundations of an effective classroom environment are built of routines, regularly repeated and reinforced. Without this essential groundwork, the edifice of learning would simply crumble.

When setting and enforcing routines, it is often tempting to focus on the big things. After all, it is hard to ignore a flagrant flouting of the rules without losing face. But the silent killer in most classrooms is low-level disruption – those seemingly minor distractions like tapping a pen, swinging on a chair, chewing gum, drawing graffiti in an exercise book, and so on. Low-level disruption is what often stymies learning because it wages a war of attrition; it corrodes the edifice of good practice we work so hard to construct.

The best way to deal with low-level disruption is to remember that it is not (usually) intended to undermine the teacher. We should, therefore, keep our cool.

Most low-level disruption arises at the beginning and end of lessons and during the transitions between tasks. It would follow, therefore, that embedding good routines for managing these transitions is – at least in part – to obviate low-level disruption. Let's take a look at each stage of the lesson.

The beginnings of lessons

We can make or break a lesson in the first few minutes. We need to establish our authority and show learners that our classroom is our domain. We might decide to make learners line up outside – at least for the first lesson – and only enter once they are silent, attentive, and have removed their coats.

Once learners have embedded the behaviours that we expect for entering our classroom and sitting down, we might want to make sure we have tasks readily displayed on the board or on desks so that learners can get started as soon as they enter. We should greet learners at the door whenever possible and do so with a smile and a quick greeting.

The best starter work is that which reviews, consolidates, or builds on the work completed in the previous lesson or lessons, and that which requires learners to revisit or revise work they had previously found difficult.

Whatever approach we take for the start of our lessons, we should always try to be in our classroom before learners arrive and have resources ready to go. If learners think we are more disorganised than they are, they will not respect us or trust us to help them make progress.

The ends of lessons

We should set clear expectations for the end of lessons, too, and manage them just as keenly as we do the beginnings: we are in charge and only we can say when the lesson has finished and learners can pack away.

It's helpful to rehearse how learners do this calmly and quietly until it becomes automatic. We might also establish routines for who leaves first in order to avoid having a mad rush out of the door. If we need to speak to learners at the end, we should try to do so quickly so as not to impair the start of the lesson for their next teacher.

Handing out books

We should explicitly teach learners how to pass out resources, including textbooks, taking a minute to explain the right way to do it (e.g., pass across rows, start on the teacher's command, only the person passing papers can get out of his or her seat, do it in silence, etc.) and allow learners time to practise until this, too, becomes automatic.

Although it may delay the start of the first lesson of the term, it is time well spent and will pay dividends later, saving time and energy for every lesson for the rest of the year and limiting the opportunity for learners to engage in low-level disruption.

Classroom discussions and debate

As well as practising handing out work, it might be worth rehearsing some of the other seemingly inconsequential activities that take place every lesson, such as transitioning from one task to another, engaging in paired talk and group work, taking part in questions-and-answers, and so on. These activities are the glue that binds the classroom together.

We might establish rules and routines for paired talk, such as how to take turns, make notes, give feedback to the class, comment on other pairs' answers, and so on. Likewise, we might get learners to practise how to work as part of a group, reinforcing what is expected of them – for example, any member of the group could be asked to give feedback, so every learner must be prepared.

Perhaps the most important routine to practise, however, is how to engage in whole-class question-and-answer sessions: here, it's helpful to make clear our rules around no-hands-up (questions will be targeted at named individuals and no one must call out) and no-excuses (everyone must give an answer), and we might practise routines such as commenting on and adding to someone else's answer in a polite and constructive manner.

Whatever routines we establish in our classrooms, we should ensure they do not disadvantage some learners because of their additional and different needs or because of their backgrounds.

Making reasonable adjustments to the classroom environment

According to a 2014 report by the charity Mencap,[1] 65% of parents of children with SEND believed their child had received a poorer quality of education than their peers without SEND, in large part because their child had sometimes been removed from the classroom and taught separately, but also because the physical, social, emotional and learning environment in their main classroom had not been adjusted to meet their needs.

In 2013, the University of London's Institute of Education[2] reported that learners with SEND were routinely segregated from their teachers and classmates, spending more than a quarter of their time in school away from qualified teachers and the classroom.

What's more, when learners with SEND *are* taken out of their normal classrooms, they tend to be housed in smaller rooms that are not as comfortable or conducive to learning. It is not atypical, for example, for these learners to be taught (either in small groups or on the basis of one-to-one tuition) in rooms which have ill-matched and broken tables and chairs and which were designed for other purposes, such as the dining hall, library, computer room, and staff offices. These rooms are, by their nature, often adjacent to busy or noisy spaces, such as staff rooms, playgrounds, or corridors, and have become dumping grounds for unused stationery or broken equipment. Sometimes, these rooms are also poorly ventilated or heated and have little natural light.

Both the Teacher Standards (2012) and the SEND Code of Practice (2014) require teachers to ensure all the learners in their classes can access learning, and this – it is made explicitly clear – means adapting their learning environment, for example, by providing visual timetables, writing frames and mind-maps, or by providing physical resources such as sloped writing boards.

Learners with SEND also tend to respond best when the classroom is tidy and organised, when the teacher sits with the learner at the front of the class and provides handouts which summarise and clarify the key points from the lesson rather than expecting learners to copy copiously from the board.

As such, in addition to what I said previously, the most effective classroom environments tend to have a range of resources such as personalised dictionaries, writing frames, lists of sentence starters, lists of linking words, mini-whiteboards and coloured pens, pastel coloured paper and notebooks, aide memoire to support individual learning activities, and tailored handouts to support specific tasks.

Learners who are susceptible to visual stress are best supported by coloured overlays, cream paper for handouts and exercise books, pastel or cream backgrounds on computer screens and PowerPoint presentations, font size no smaller than 12 point for paper and 28 point for PowerPoint, texts in a sans serif font such as Arial, Verdana, Tahoma, and Comic Sans, left-justified text, and the use of bold to emphasise text but the avoidance of italics, underlining and capitals.

Classroom displays work best for learners with SEND when they are informative, interactive, and relevant, are uncluttered so that key information can quickly and easily be found, and can be seen from every position in the classroom. Displays also work best when there is a good use of colour, when they contain keywords that are explicitly taught to and understood by all learners and then frequently referenced in lessons, and when they celebrate learners' work and make them feel valued.

The classroom environments that work best for learners with SEND are also:

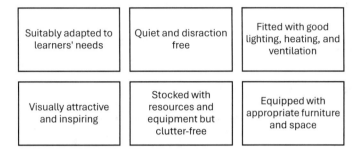

Figure 8.1 Features of a SEND classroom environment

The SEND Code of Practice says that "Special educational provision is underpinned by high quality teaching and is compromised by anything less". Providing an inclusive classroom environment whereby learners' needs are met without drawing attention to their difficulties is therefore crucial because this will maximise their potential but limit any feelings they may have of embarrassment and frustration.

With this in mind, here are some practical tips for:

- Supporting learners with memory difficulties
- Teaching spelling
- Teaching reading
- Teaching writing
- Teaching through intervention

Supporting learners with SEND who have memory difficulties

When supporting learners with memory difficulties, we might:

- Revisit previous learning at the beginning of the lesson, allowing learners to recall and make associations with new learning.
- Give an overview of the lesson so the learners can see the outcome and make sense of the content.
- Revisit learning at regular intervals throughout the lesson.
- 'Chunk' new information and regularly check understanding.

- Use a step-by-step approach to completing any task with regular checkpoints for monitoring progress and giving feedback.

- When giving instructions, limit the number, repeat them, and provide notes and a checklist.

- Use simple, concise sentences when giving direct instruction.

- Consider the pace of delivery – speak more slowly if necessary.

- Use songs, rhyme, and rap to aid memorisation.

- Allow 'wait time' for learners to process information before articulating an answer.

- Allow learners to work collaboratively.

- Ensure that the tasks are relevant to the learning and eliminate those that will interfere with that learning, such as copying from the board or writing the date and title.

- When learners are on task, avoid interrupting their learning.

- At the end of the lesson, summarise the learning and say what the next lesson will be about.

- Paint the big picture for learners, showing how each lesson fits in and builds upon the last.

Supporting learners with SEND to improve their spelling

When teaching spelling, we might:

- Provide subject-specific keywords in handouts.

- Encourage learners to take risks with their spelling, suggesting that they underline these words.

- Encourage a metacognitive approach by asking learners to analyse their spelling mistakes and identify the learning required.

Supporting learners with SEND to improve their reading skills

When teaching reading, we might:

- Only ask a learner to read aloud if we know they want to.

- Ensure that books are at the right level of difficulty for learners.

- Use audiobooks when appropriate.

- Teach reading skills, such as skimming, scanning, and close reading.

- Encourage learners to condense and make sense of what they read, for example, by making mind maps and drawing diagrams and flow charts.

- Explicitly teach key vocabulary learners will encounter in the text before they start reading.

- Encourage learners to question the writer's techniques and intentions and consider their own views and experiences in relation to the text.

- Instil in learners a desire to read by providing reading materials that are of interest to them.

Supporting learners with SEND to improve their writing skills

When teaching writing, we might:

- Check learners' understanding of the task before they begin writing.

- Use technology such as voice recognition software or mind mapping software to improve written outcomes.

- Provide examples and model good practice whilst thinking aloud.

- Break down a writing task into manageable chunks.

- Teach, model, and encourage learners to plan.

- Give specific feedback at each stage so learners know what to repeat or improve.

- Provide a mix of written and verbal feedback.

- Improve proofreading by building in proofreading time in lessons, using a 'buddying' system, teaching and modelling strategies, providing proofreading checklists, encouraging learners to read work aloud, and leaving 'thinking time' between writing and proofreading.

Supporting learners with SEND through intervention

When teaching through additional interventions, we might:

- Ensure lessons are structured, cumulative, and multi-sensory.

- Ensure the learner governs the pace of delivery.

- Ensure the specific needs of the learner are met.

- Ensure the knowledge and skills taught in the intervention session are transferred back to the classroom.

- Ensure progress is reviewed and tracked at regular intervals.

- Ensure the learner enjoys the learning and feels motivated, confident, and self-empowered.

Attending to the physical, social and emotional environments

I'm sure each of us has a set of personal preferences with regards to our immediate environments. We are each of us comforted by certain conditions and discomforted by others –

whether it's light, heat and noise, or more tangible features (some of us like order and organisation, perhaps to the point of sparsity; others like clutter and chaos and feel safe when surrounded by their hordes). And this is only the physical environment; there are also the social and emotional environments to consider. Some people (and misery) like company; others like solitude. Some people like a buoyant, busy atmosphere; others library-like quietude. And what applies to the home also applies at school – so, what of the school environment? What physical, social, and emotional conditions are most conducive to learning? And what may distract learners from their work?

Although each learner is different, we know that the quality of the learning environment matters and that learners need to feel comfortable if they are to accept the challenge of hard work, and their basic needs must be met if they are to attend to the curriculum.

How we use our classroom space and the rules, routines, and expectations we establish are, therefore, crucial considerations. Let's look at the features of an effective physical environment first.

The physical environment

The physical environment refers to the concrete aspects of our surroundings that affect our senses – the quality of the school buildings, the attractiveness and usefulness of classroom walls, the quality of light and the temperature, and to how the physical space is utilised.

Research by the University of Salford[3] suggests that learners' emotional and physiological stability can directly impact on their understanding of the school curriculum and, therefore, affect the pace of their progress. Creating a physical environment that allows learners to feel comfortable, content, and focused can help them become more attentive to the teacher and more attuned to the content of the curriculum they are studying. In other words, learners' conscious and subconscious attention and the development of their knowledge, skills, and understandings are more effectively piqued when they study in a positive physical space.

The University of Salford study suggests that a wide range of environmental factors can contribute towards the emotional and physiological effects of a classroom. For example, environmental factors, including natural light, noise, classroom orientation, temperature, and even air quality, have been shown to improve learners' achievement by as much as 25% in an academic year. Salford also found that over 70% of the variations in learner performance could be directly attributed to environmental factors.

Emotional factors can be just as significant as physical ones when it comes to improving learners' capacity to learn and their intellectual understanding of the curriculum. What's more, the first few days spent in a new learning environment are the most pivotal in determining a learner's academic progress. We need only look at the effects of a learner's transition from primary to secondary school – whereby, according to Galton,[4] almost 40% of children fail to make expected progress – to see this. If a learner does not feel emotionally safe and intellectually comfortable, it can prove difficult for them to make progress.

Of course, classrooms should always be a safe place for learners wherein they feel supported physically, emotionally, and academically. This support comes not just from teachers but also from their peers, support staff, and the physical classroom itself. An intelligently designed physical school environment with, for example, distinct and clear lines of communication can help promote dialogue between learners and teachers. This, in turn, can help learners feel better integrated into the learning process which, in turn, helps promote wellbeing within the classroom.

Light is critical for our health and wellbeing. Ensuring that we receive adequate light levels at the appropriate time of day benefits our alertness, mood, productivity, sleep patterns and many aspects of our physiology. Furthermore, the use of colour in the classroom can affect learners' moods and emotional wellbeing. Ancient Chinese and Egyptian civilisations practiced the early arts of chromotherapy, which involved the use of colours as therapy and emotional healing, a practice that is still widely used today.

Creating a positive physical environment, then, is crucial to ensuring every learner is included and makes progress, but environmental factors become even more critical to learners' success when those learners have additional needs or disadvantages.

Here are my top tips for creating an effective physical classroom environment:

Displays

There is a balance to be struck here, I think. We do not want bare walls because such a stark environment is uninspiring and can be demotivating. But likewise, we do not want the walls to be so engaging as to distract learners from the lesson or offend their eyes with a kaleidoscope of colour and shape. If we do have displays, we want them to be useful and useable, not mere wallpaper, and we want them to be up-to-date and relevant, not formed of peeling and yellowed posters from yesteryear.

We should think carefully, therefore, about what would prove most useful to most learners who study in the room, what would provide cues for their learning, and what would act as schema or stimulants to thought. For example, we may want to display keywords or concepts, perhaps threshold curriculum content or ideas from knowledge organisers. Consistency may also be helpful here so that learners know where to look in each classroom for key information.

Light and heat

Maslow's hierarchy of needs is widely known, and we can't ignore the importance of catering to our learners' more basic needs because if they are uncomfortable, they are less likely to concentrate in lessons. It's important to consider any individual needs, such as those outlined in learners' education, health, and care plans (EHCPs), as well as to refer to SEND law and best practice, particularly for learners with sensory difficulties.

According to research, classroom lighting also plays a critical role in both learner performance and staff wellbeing (see Phillips 1997). Jago and Tanner (1999) cite the results of 17 studies from the mid-1930s to 1997. The consensus of these studies is that appropriate lighting improves test scores, reduces off-task behaviour, and plays a significant role in the achievement of learners.[5]

Noise

Another physical condition of importance to both learner success and staff wellbeing pertains to noise levels.

Earthman and Lemasters (1997)[6] report that higher learner achievement is associated with schools that have less external noise, outside noise causes increased learner dissatisfaction with their classrooms, and excessive noise causes stress in learners.

Layout

Sometimes, it is best for learners to be seated in rows facing the teacher and the board; other times, if it's logistically possible and not time-consuming, it may be best to deviate from this layout to facilitate discussion and debate or to allow safe movement around the classroom.

Seating in rows focuses learners on the teacher and whiteboard and, therefore, minimises distractions and low-level disruption. What's more, it enables the teacher to see all their learners all of the time.

The social and emotional environments

Once we have catered for our learners' basic needs and created a physical environment in which they are comfortable and focused on learning, we need to consider the social environment.

An effective social environment, at least in part, means a whole school culture which is conducive to good behaviour and attitudes to learning, tackles poor behaviour, including low-level disruption, and protects all staff and learners from harassment and harm. This is, as I have already explained, about establishing a set of social norms. But it's also much more than this. As well as building a comfortable and engaging physical space and developing appropriate behaviours and attitudes – and indeed routines – towards learning, we want our learners to feel safe and secure in school so that they willingly take risks and make mistakes from which they can learn.

As such, here are five practical strategies to help instil a willingness to take risks – what we might refer to as a 'growth mindset' – in the classroom.

Figure 8.2 Features of a growth mindset classroom

1. Frequent formative feedback

The first strategy to help develop the sort of emotional environment that encourages risk-taking is to provide learners with frequent formative feedback. Dr Carol Dweck, in her book *Mindset*,[7] argues that people with a fixed mindset "greatly mis-estimated their performance and their ability [while] people with the growth mindset were amazingly accurate" (p. 6). Why should this be? Because, as Dr Dweck says:

> If, like those with the growth mindset, you believe you can develop yourself, then you're open to accurate information about your current abilities, even if it's unflattering. What's more, if you're oriented towards learning, as they are, you need accurate information about your current abilities in order to learn effectively.
>
> (p. 3)

We should, therefore, ensure that our learners are acutely aware of their strengths and areas for development. We should frequently assess our learners and give them formative feedback so that they know what they do well and what they can do better. We should dedicate quality time in our lessons for our learners to act on this feedback and to redraft work in order to improve upon it.

2. High levels of challenge for all

Everyone can improve with practice. Therefore, we must challenge our learners to be the best they can be; we must have high expectations of all our learners and must encourage them to take a leap of faith, even if that means falling over a few times. Appropriate challenge – and high expectations – are not just advisable; they are essential to the process of learning. If learners are not given hard work to do which makes them think, they won't learn anything. Likewise, we know from the work of Rosenthal and Jacobson[8] that having high expectations of learners demonstrably improves their outcomes. Conversely, if we set the bar low, learners are likely to underperform.

It's important, therefore, that our emotional environment is built on high expectations and the provision of stretch and challenge for all learners.

3. Mistakes explicitly welcomed

Another way of developing an emotional environment that encourages risk-taking is to actively encourage learners to make mistakes, and to do this, we must foster a safe and secure environment in which falling over is not only accepted without criticism or humiliation but in which it is actively encouraged as evidence of effective learning and of getting better at something.

We all know that some learners do not proactively contribute in class or answer a question because they fear they will be criticised or made to feel embarrassed for being wrong. And yet, the opposite should be true: learners should be eager to engage because to get an answer wrong is to learn from their mistakes; to get an answer wrong is to learn the correct answer.

86 Why School Doesn't Work for Every Child

Equally, admitting 'I don't understand this . . . can you help?' is not a sign of weakness or low intelligence; it is a means of increasing one's intelligence.

Of course, making a mistake – even if you have a positive mindset – can be a painful experience. But a mistake shouldn't define us; it's a problem to be faced and learned from. We can teach this by modelling it, by publicly making mistakes, and by making explicit our own implicit learning.

An effective emotional environment, therefore, is one in which mistakes are welcomed and learned from.

4. Opportunities for retrieval practice

In his book *Outliers*,[9] Malcolm Gladwell suggests that as a society, we value natural, effortless accomplishments over achievement through effort. We endow our heroes with superhuman abilities that lead them inevitably towards greatness. People with a belief in the growth mindset and an eagerness to take risks and learn from mistakes, however, believe something very different. For them, even geniuses must work hard for their achievements. After all, what's heroic about having a gift?

Matthew Syed, author of *Bounce*,[10] quantifies the amount of 'purposeful practice' that is required to achieve excellence. He says that "from art to science and from board games to tennis, it has been found that a minimum of ten years is required to reach world-class status in any complex task".

We should, therefore, provide our learners with plenty of opportunities to practise and perfect their knowledge and skills.

Retrieval practice protects against forgetting and improves transfer.

There are two kinds of retrieval practice proven to be the most effective: distributed practice, which is "a schedule of practice that spreads out study activities over time"; and interleaved practice, which is "a schedule of practice that mixes different kinds of problems, or a schedule of study that mixes different kinds of material, within a single study session" (Dunlosky et al, 2013).[11]

An effective emotional environment, therefore, is one which provides learners with plentiful opportunities to engage in deliberate practice, both to activate prior learning and keep it accessible and to ensure that they continue to improve.

5. Rewards for effort, not attainment

Returning to Dr Dweck for a moment, she conducted research into the effects of rewards and concluded that praising learners' abilities lowered their IQs, whereas praising effort improved them.

Dweck also found that praising learners' intelligence can harm their motivation because, although learners love to be praised, especially for their talents, as soon as they hit a snag, their confidence dissipates, and their motivation dies.

This doesn't mean we shouldn't praise learners, of course. But it does mean that an effective emotional environment is one in which we use praise carefully and predominantly praise learners for the 'growth-oriented process' – what Dweck describes as "what they accomplished through practice, study, persistence, and good strategies", whilst avoiding the kind of praise that judges their intelligence or talent.

Notes

1 https://www.mencap.org.uk/sites/default/files/2016-06/annual_report_2014_v12_AD.pdf
2 https://assets.publishing.service.gov.uk/government/uploads/system/uploads/attachment_data/file/351496/RR354_-_Students__educational_and_developmental_outcomes_at_age_16.pdf
3 http://www.salford.ac.uk/business/consultancy/case-studies-nightingale-schools
4 https://www.researchgate.net/publication/241563201_The_Impact_of_School_Transitions_on_Pupil_Progress_and_Attainment
5 Buckley, J., Schneider, M., & Shang, L. (2004). *The effects of school facility on teacher retention in urban school districts*. Boston College and Stony Brook University.
6 As per previous footnote.
7 Dweck, C. (2007). *Mindset: The new psychology of success*. Random House.
8 Rosenthal, R., & Jacobson, L. (1968). *Pygmalion in the classroom: Teacher expectation and student intellectual development* (p. 47). Holt, Rinehart & Winston.
9 Gladwell, M. (2008). *Outliers: The story of success*. Penguin.
10 Syed, M. (2011). *Bounce: The myth of talent and the power of practice*. Fourth Estate.
11 Dunlosky, J., Rawson, K.A., Marsh, E.J., Nathan, M.J., & Willingham, D.T. (2013). Improving students' learning with effective learning techniques: Promising directions from cognitive and educational psychology. *Psychological Science in the Public Interest, 14*(1), 4–58. https://doi.org/10.1177/1529100612453266

9 Behaviour skills and consequences

3 Skilled staff

As I explained earlier, behaviour management is not solely in the domain of the classroom teacher. Rather, it is for school leaders to establish a whole-school culture of high expectations. Such a culture is built of routines, repeatedly reinforced. And such a culture is built of effective systems and structures, including for the provision of rewards and sanctions.

But, once we've established such a culture, it's important to provide school staff with training that equips them with the skills they need to manage learner behaviour in their classrooms.

The Great Teaching Toolkit from Evidence Based Education[1] says that effective teachers create a supportive learning environment. Such an environment, they say, is characterised by "relationships of trust and respect between students and teachers, and among students. It is one in which students are motivated, supported and challenged and have a positive attitude towards their learning".

This is achieved in four ways by:

1. Promoting interactions and relationships with all learners that are based on mutual respect, care, empathy, and warmth; avoiding negative emotions in interactions with learners; being sensitive to the individual needs, emotions, culture, and beliefs of learners.

2. Promoting a positive climate of learner-to-learner relationships characterised by respect, trust, cooperation, and care.

3. Promoting learner motivation through feelings of competence, autonomy, and relatedness.

4. Creating a climate of high expectations with high challenge and high trust so learners feel it is okay to have a go. Encouraging learners to attribute their success or failure to things they can change.

Effective teachers, says the toolkit, also maximise opportunities to learn: "Managing the behaviour and activities of a class of students is what teachers do".

The toolkit offers three methods for maximising opportunities to learn:

1. Managing time and resources efficiently in the classroom to maximise productivity and minimise wasted time (e.g., lesson starts, ends, and transitions); giving clear instructions so learners understand what they should be doing; using (and explicitly teaching) routines to make transitions smooth.

2. Ensuring that rules, expectations, and consequences for behaviour are explicit, clear, and consistently applied.

3. Preventing, anticipating, and responding to potentially disruptive incidents; reinforcing positive learner behaviours; signalling awareness of what is happening in the classroom and responding appropriately.

The behaviour checklists produced by Charlie Taylor in 2011 for the DfE[2] offer further practical advice for teachers when it comes to managing behaviour in their classrooms.

Taylor says,

Where there is inconsistency, children are more likely to push the boundaries. If a pupil thinks there is a chance that [a teacher] will forget about the detention he has been given, then he is unlikely to bother to turn up. If he gets away with it, the threat of detention will be no deterrent in the future.

Often it is doing the simple things that can make a difference with behaviour . . . . For example, the teacher who takes the time to meet and greet pupils at the door will find they come in happier and ready to learn.

Teachers who follow these guidelines find there is more consistency in approach to managing behaviour. When children know that teachers will stick to the behaviour policy and class routines, they feel safer and happy, and behaviour improves.

Taylor's advice for teachers is as follows:

Classroom

- Know the names and roles of any adults in class.

- Meet and greet learners when they come into the classroom.

- Display rules in the class – and ensure that the learners and staff know what they are.

- Display the tariff of sanctions in class.

- Have a system in place to follow through with all sanctions.

- Display the tariff of rewards in class.

- Have a system in place to follow through with all rewards.

90 Why School Doesn't Work for Every Child

- Have a visual timetable on the wall.

- Follow the school behaviour policy.

Learners

- Know the names of learners.

- Have a plan for children who are likely to misbehave.

- Ensure other adults in the class know the plan.

- Understand learners' special needs.

Teaching

- Ensure that all resources are prepared in advance.

- Praise the behaviour you want to see more of.

- Praise children doing the right thing more than you criticise those doing the wrong thing (parallel praise).

- Differentiate.

- Stay calm.

- Have clear routines for transitions and for stopping the class.

- Teach children the class routines.

One way to ensure learners learn from their mistakes and behave more appropriately in future is to explicitly teach metacognitive strategies so that they become more self-regulated as learners.

Teaching metacognition

Metacognition is what learners *know* about learning, whereas self-regulation is what learners *do* about learning. Self-regulation describes how learners monitor and control their cognitive processes – which, I would argue, includes their behaviour. Put another way, self-regulated learners are aware of their strengths and weaknesses and can motivate themselves to engage in and improve their learning. This applies to how they conduct themselves in the classroom and how they respond when they feel under threat or when they are bored or stuck.

One way to teach learners how to become more self-regulated is to model the thinking processes of a self-regulated person by thinking aloud and making explicit how we, as teachers and adults, monitor and control our responses to threatening situations. For example, we could model how we deal with our 'fight or flight' response, which is a battle between our limbic system (which is the primitive part of our brain, sometimes called the 'chimp', that responds intuitively and emotionally to situations) and our frontal lobe (which is often referred to as 'the human' part of the brain, or the computer, because it developed much later as we acquired the art of logic, of thinking through situations rationally, predicting a range of possible outcomes and making informed decisions).

It's important we remember this internal battle when tackling low-level disruption (controlling our own fight or flight response) *and* when understanding why a learner has sought to disrupt the class (helping them to control their inner chimp). For example, to help learners, we can teach them to actively acknowledge the chimp's existence and make it a habit, whenever conflict arises, to pause before responding to it. There's a reason we are counselled to 'count to ten' whenever we're irritated or angered, after all. We can also teach learners – through modelling – to apologise when their limbic system gets the better of them – as it sometimes will because they're human and fallible – and acknowledge the way they responded was inappropriate and unhelpful, then seek to learn from it.

We'll return to metacognition in more detail later.

Seven strategies for classroom management

Here are seven strategies that teachers can employ to prevent low-level disruption or to handle it better when it happens:

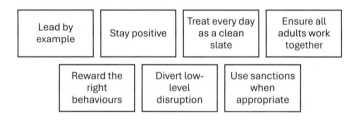

Figure 9.1 Seven classroom management strategies

Firstly, we can **lead by example**. In other words, at the start of the lesson, we can stand at the door smiling in order to show the class that we are enthusiastic about teaching them and that our classroom is a happy, friendly place to learn. We can greet each learner with a smile and a friendly 'hello' as they enter the room. Such an approach not only shows our class that we enjoy teaching them and will treat each learner as an individual; it also models the way we expect our learners to behave.

Secondly, we can **stay positive**. We can try our best to avoid using negative words or body language and remember we're not there to judge learners. When we need to discipline a learner, we can try to distinguish between their behaviour and them as a person – it is the behaviour that was inappropriate, not the learner. By staying positive, we are once again modelling the types of behaviours we expect from learners – we are showing that we expect them, too, to stay in control of their emotions. We can also try to remain polite, saying 'thank you' to learners and making sure that every learner (even the quiet ones) is acknowledged for their contributions to the lesson.

Thirdly, we can **treat every day as a clean slate**. We can ensure that incidents are dealt with and, where possible, resolved by the end of the day on which they take place. The next day should be a fresh start for everyone: we can make clear through our choice of words and body language that those learners who misbehaved yesterday are starting today with a clean slate. We can begin the day with high expectations for every learner – each new day is a new start.

Fourthly, we can **ensure all the adults in the classroom work together**. If we have another adult working with us in the classroom, such as a teaching assistant, we can make sure we have agreed with them in advance on how we will tackle behaviour matters. We need to ensure we both speak with one voice and are certain the other will support and mirror our actions and decisions. If the adults in the room have different ways of approaching behaviour management and are seen to disagree about how to discipline learners, not only does this send mixed signals to learners, but it also paves the way for learners to argue with us and try to drive a wedge between the adults.

Fifthly, we can **reward the right behaviours**, giving oxygen to those who deserve it most. Often, the best way of dealing with inappropriate behaviour is through the positive reinforcement of good behaviours. Not only does rewarding good behaviour ensure that those learners who behave well and work hard receive recognition for their efforts, but it also models for those learners who misbehave exactly what is expected of them, too. Praise for good behaviour and good work should be sincere and appropriate to the age and ability of the learner.

Sixthly, we can try to **divert low-level disruptions**. If poor behaviour becomes disruptive to the learning, we can try to divert it in an unobtrusive manner, such as by using eye contact or questions to distract learners who are misbehaving and to make them aware we have noticed their misbehaviour and now want them to refocus on the lesson. If poor behaviour continues, we can try to find a way to prevent it, such as changing our seating plan or altering the way in which our classroom is set up. If necessary, we can talk to the learner about their behaviour and make clear that it falls below the standard we expect of them – and, crucially, that their behaviour falls below the standard we know they can produce. Notwithstanding this, we still need to be firm and make sure that the learner understands they have been warned; we need to make sure they know the consequences of any further disruption

Finally, we should not be afraid to **use sanctions when appropriate**. We should always follow the school's policy for managing behaviour, including in our use of rewards and sanctions. When sanctions have been used, we can make sure the learner is later afforded the time and opportunity to rectify their mistakes and to make choices about their future behaviour. We can try to catch them doing the right thing and give them positive feedback. When we apply the sanction, we can do so with empathy and patience, show we care about the learner, and are disappointed that we have been left with no option but to use a sanction.

Putting it into practice

Here are my top five tips for putting classroom management skills into practice:

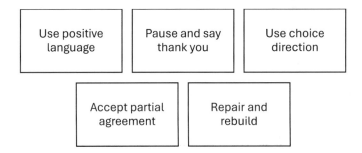

Figure 9.2 Five behaviour management strategies

1. Use positive language

- Instead of saying, "Will you stop talking", say, "I'd like everyone listening".
- Instead of saying, "Stop turning around", say, "I'd like everyone facing this way, thank you".

2. Pause and say thank you

- First, get learners' attention with a direction and eye contact . . .
- Second, make a deliberate pause . . .
- Third, give an instruction, chunked if necessary . . .
- Fourth, make another deliberate pause to ensure sufficient 'take-up' time.

Here's an example:

> "Everyone . . . [pause] . . . face this way . . . [pause] . . . and listen . . . [pause] . . . thank you".

Note:

- It's better to say "thank you" than "please" because this assumes compliance with the request; it's more assertive.

3. Use choice direction

- Say *Either/or*: "Either you can work quietly by yourself, or you can come up and sit with me".
- Say *When/then*: "When you have finished this task, then you can chat with your neighbour".

4. Accept partial agreement

- As the adult, a teacher should model positive behaviours by not escalating a situation – sometimes, that means not having the last word.

94 Why School Doesn't Work for Every Child

Here's an example:

Learner: I wasn't talking, I was doing my work.

Teacher: Okay, maybe you were, but now I want you to press on and finish the task.

Learner: It wasn't me . . . I didn't do anything.

Teacher: Maybe not. But we're all clear on the rules about that, aren't we? And I'd like you to help me out next time. Thank you.

- Expecting compliance is key, but we should not regard 'giving in' as a weakness. Saying to learners that we may be wrong is a good way to model positive behaviours and an important part of building relationships whilst maintaining our authority.

5. Repair and rebuild

- Teachers are human, too, and sometimes we get things wrong – when we do, we should acknowledge our emotions (e.g., "I got angry because . . .").
- Then, after cooling down, we should model the behaviours we want to see.

Reasonable adjustments to classroom management

This book is about building equity in education. It would be remiss of me, therefore, not to mention the importance of making reasonable adjustments to our behaviour policies and practices for those learners with additional needs and who face challenges when conforming to our expectations.

To be clear, schools are only expected to make reasonable adjustments for learners with disabilities as defined under the Equality Act 2010, but the legal position does not always equate to the moral one. I believe schools have an ethical duty to ensure that every learner – no matter their starting points, backgrounds, differences, and disadvantages – has a right to an education, and that means doing all we can to make school accessible and inclusive; it means doing all we can to ensure that school does not prove a barrier to a learner's chances of success.

Making reasonable adjustments to our behaviour policies and practices does not mean reducing our expectations or accepting inappropriate behaviour from some learners, nor does it mean having one rule for some and another rule for others. As I have said, an effective whole-school culture promotes high standards of behaviour for all. But an effective culture is also one that provides the necessary support to ensure all learners can achieve and thrive both in and out of the classroom.

Therefore, we need to consider how our whole-school approach to behaviour meets the needs of all learners in our school, including learners with SEND and those from a disadvantage, so that everyone feels that they belong. Indeed, this is the key: belonging.

Schools with effective behaviour cultures create safe, calm, and supportive environments which benefit all learners.

A starting point for making reasonable adjustments is an understanding that some behaviours are more likely to be associated with particular types of SEND. For example, a learner with speech, language, and communication needs (SLCN) is more likely to find it difficult to understand a verbal instruction and, therefore, will face greater challenges responding to it. Of course, this is not to say that every incident of misbehaviour will be connected to a learner's SEND.

The graduated approach

When a learner is identified as having SEND, we should apply the graduated approach that I mentioned earlier in this book. Here's a reminder:

Figure 9.3 The graduated approach

UK law also requires schools to balance several duties which have a bearing on behaviour policies and practice, particularly where a learner has SEND that at times affects their behaviour. In particular, schools have a duty under the Equality Act 2010 to "take such steps as is reasonable to avoid any substantial disadvantage to a disabled pupil caused by the school's policies or practices". Schools have a duty under the Children and Families Act 2014 to "use their 'best endeavours' to meet the needs of those with SEND". Further, if a learner has an Education, Health, and Care Plan (EHCP), then the provisions set out in that plan must be secured, and the school must cooperate with the local authority and other bodies.

Government advice, contained in a document entitled Behaviour in Schools,[3] says that "as part of meeting any of these duties, schools should, as far as possible, anticipate likely triggers of misbehaviour and put in place support to prevent these".

The document proffers the following illustrative examples of preventative measures:

- Short, planned movement breaks for a learner whose SEND means that they find it difficult to sit still for long

- Adjusting seating plans to allow a learner with visual or hearing impairment to sit in sight of the teacher

- Adjusting uniform requirements for a learner with sensory issues or who has severe eczema
- Training for staff in understanding conditions such as autism

4 A clear system of consequences

Three layers of behaviour management

Broadly speaking, behaviour management strategies fall into three categories:

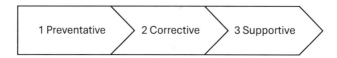

Figure 9.4 Three layers of behaviour management

1. **Preventative:** Those strategies which prevent misbehaviour from occurring, including being clear about what is expected of learners and what will happen if those expectations are not met.

2. **Corrective:** Those strategies which correct misbehaviour once it has occurred, including making clear that a learner has misbehaved and sanctioning them.

3. **Supportive:** Those strategies that involve working with a learner after they have misbehaved in order to identify why they misbehaved and how they can avoid doing so again.

Preventative behaviour management is about having a learner contract or a clear set of rules which are known and understood by learners. It is about having a clear set of rewards and sanctions to encourage good behaviour and dissuade learners from misbehaving. However, it is also about how the classroom is organised: using an appropriate seating plan, having appropriate activities which challenge and support in equal measure, having appropriate pace and variety, and having the right resources. And it is about how the curriculum and timetable are organised: making sure learning pathways are appropriate for every learner and that there is an alternative curriculum for those who cannot access or are not motivated by the traditional curriculum. Finally, preventative behaviour management is about reinforcing the rules as often as possible.

Corrective behaviour management is about the teacher reinforcing what is expected of learners in every lesson, being consistent in how they discipline learners, and being fair in applying sanctions. Corrective behaviour management is also about following up on incidents.

Supportive behaviour management is about what happens after the teacher has corrected a learner's behaviour. It is about exploring why a learner misbehaved in the first place to avoid a repeat. It is about setting out what is expected of the learner next and about agreeing that next time the sanction will be different (the next stage up) and/or agreeing on a means of avoiding misbehaviour (e.g., a 'time-out' card, a mentor, counselling, etc.).

The importance of consequences

With rights come responsibilities. And with actions come consequences. Having an effective system of rewards and sanctions is not only important to maintaining order in school, but it also teaches learners crucial life lessons. It's important that learners know what is expected of them and what will happen if they fail to meet those expectations. Rules, rewards, and sanctions provide clear boundaries that help make learners feel safe, add to the predictability of the classroom, and help prevent disruption. Often, disadvantaged learners and those with additional needs find themselves in lower sets where there is a higher prevalence of misbehaviour. Rewards and sanctions are, therefore, even more impactful for these learners.

As I said earlier in this chapter, we should always try to reward the right behaviours and thus give oxygen to those who deserve it most. As a rule of thumb, I'd recommend working on a ratio of three rewards to every sanction. By analysing behaviour data, we could hold true to that balance. As I also said earlier, one of the best ways of dealing with misbehaviour is by using rewards to positively reinforce good behaviours, thereby modelling for those learners who misbehave exactly what is expected of them.

We should not be afraid to use sanctions when appropriate, but when we do, we should also make sure that the learner is afforded the time and opportunity to rectify their mistakes and to make choices about their future behaviour. We should also try to catch them doing the right thing and give them positive feedback for it. And we should apply sanctions with empathy and patience – this might mean taking time to listen to the learner and find out why they misbehaved and what support they need to avoid a repeat. Listening to learners and taking a respectful approach to behaviour management is not the same as having low expectations or tolerating misbehaviour; it does not have to run counter to a 'no excuses' policy.

One way to make a success of a rewards and sanctions system is to analyse the data to see whether or not sanctions are leading to a reduction in misbehaviour and whether the number of sanctions issued to the same learner and for the same offence is going down over time. Put simply, if the same learners are being punished in the same way for the same offences, then the sanction probably isn't working. And, what's more, if disadvantaged learners and those with additional needs are being sanctioned far more than their peers, then this might suggest our system isn't inclusive, or our expectations are not achievable for all and that we need to make more reasonable adjustments.

Another way to make a success of rewards and sanctions is to try to understand why learners misbehave in the first place. For this, I'd posit three answers:

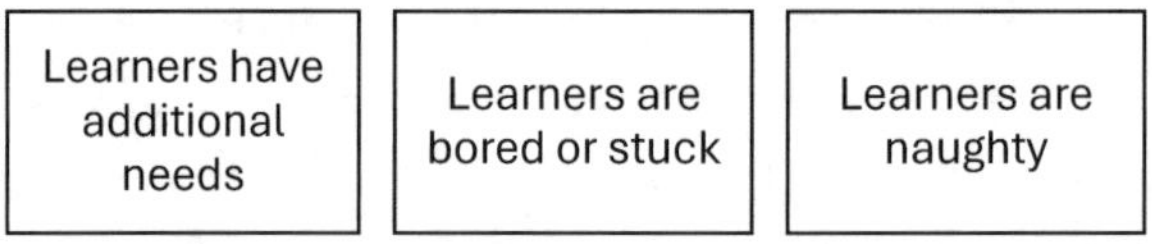

98 Why School Doesn't Work for Every Child

Learners have additional needs	Learners are bored or stuck	Learners are naughty

Figure 9.5 Reasons for misbehaviour

If a learner has additional needs that make it difficult for them to conform to our behaviour expectations, then we must make reasonable adjustments to help them access school life and make them feel like they belong. Inclusion is all about changing the school environment so that every learner is included in and feels a part of that environment.

If a learner is bored or stuck, the curriculum isn't working for them. The pitch is wrong. The solution? Better understanding learners' starting points and needs and planning a curriculum that is highly challenging but made accessible through the use of adaptive teaching strategies. The use of frequent formative assessment lies at the heart of this.

If a learner is naughty, they know how to behave and can behave but choose not to, either to gain attention or to protest at something. The solution? Making effective use of rewards and sanctions so that learners are reminded of the rules and face the consequences of their deliberate actions. Learners who can behave but choose not to will respond to a 'no excuses' approach which consists of clear rules and routines within a framework that emphasises choice and learner voice and which makes use of a tailored rewards and sanctions system.

Returning to the first group of learners – those who have additional needs – it's worth noting that some of these children will not possess the social and emotional skills needed to comply with our social norms and expectations, and so will not respond to sanctions in the long term. Put simply, we can't sanction a child for not doing something that they didn't know how to do in the first place. If a learner can't do multiplication, we teach them how to multiply. Therefore, if a learner cannot manage their emotions appropriately, we need to teach them how to recognise, explain, and manage their emotions, thus helping them become more self-aware. We need to teach them how to put themselves in other people's shoes, thus helping them become more empathetic. And we need to teach them how to develop the social skills required for group situations and to form friendships.

Of course, it's not always binary – that learners either do or don't possess the social and emotional skills needed. Rather, some learners will possess the skills but will struggle to use them in every situation. For example, some learners will find it hard to manage their emotions in stressful situations or when under duress. These learners need pastoral support, someone to talk to when things get too much, and a quiet place to go when they need time out.

Whilst accepting that high expectations are important and that all schools need robust consequences systems to ensure the safety of all learners and to help prepare all learners for future success, we must never lose sight of the fact that some learners will be suffering trauma, perhaps because they have never felt loved and protected, listened to or cared for. These children need our love and support, our patience and kindness, and specialist help, not punishment.

Here are some final tips for making a success of our consequences system:

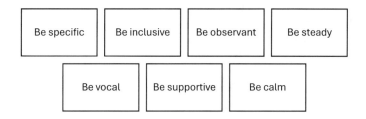

Figure 9.6 Strategies for making a success of a consequences system

Be specific

Be clear and concrete about the behaviours we expect in different situations.

Be inclusive

Use 'we' not 'you' (e.g., "At this school, we listen to others with respect").

Be observant

Look for examples of appropriate behaviours and celebrate them as models to follow.

Be steady

Give instructions in small steps, chunking information into bite-sized pieces and allowing sufficient 'take-up' time before moving on.

Be vocal

Give ongoing feedback about how learners are doing, narrating the progress they're making and feeding back on the good behaviours we see.

Be supportive

Help learners to self-regulate, prompting them with reflective questions that encourage them to monitor the amount of work they're doing and the progress they're making.

Be calm

Always avoid raising your voice, getting angry, using sarcasm, or belittling and humiliating learners. It's not the behaviour we want to model for others, and it will be counterproductive.

Notes

1 https://www.greatteaching.com
2 https://www.gov.uk/government/news/simple-behaviour-checklist-to-help-teachers-maintain-discipline-in-school
3 https://assets.publishing.service.gov.uk/media/65ce3721e1bdec001a3221fe/Behaviour_in_schools_-_advice_for_headteachers_and_school_staff_Feb_2024.pdf

 Behaviours for learning

 5 Personal development

The purpose of education

What is the purpose of education? Is it to prepare learners for the world of work or is it to instil in them an appreciation of the arts and sciences? Is it to develop character traits – such as resilience and empathy – to increase a learner's employability, or is it to indoctrinate young people into our shared culture and history? Is education a means to an end, or learning for learning's sake?

Thomas Gradgrind, the headmaster in Charles Dickens' novel *Hard Times*,[1] famously said:

> Teach these boys and girls nothing but Facts. Facts alone are wanted in life. Plant nothing else and root out everything else. You can only form the minds of reasoning animals upon Facts: nothing else will ever be of any service to them.

It's hard to deny that teaching facts is important, but surely, we shouldn't just teach facts because facts learned in isolation are of limited value. Rather, we should teach facts and then teach learners how to apply those facts in a range of different contexts and make myriad connections between them. Teaching learners how to convey their learning from one context to another is the difference between educating someone and simply training them to perform a task repeatedly.

For my part, whilst I believe that education is about teaching facts and teaching learners how to apply those facts in a range of different contexts, as well as making connections between them, I also think that education is about creating new connections. In other words, education is not just about passing on existing knowledge, but it is also about creating new knowledge and forging new understandings. Plutarch (or was it Socrates or WB Yeats? There's some confusion over attribution – ah, the limitations of facts!) put it best when he said that education was not about the filling of a pail but about the lighting of a fire.

According to Gert Biesta in his book *The Beautiful Risk of Education*,[2] there are at least three domains in which education can function and, thus, three domains in which educational purposes can be articulated. One is the domain of *qualification*, which is concerned with the acquisition of knowledge, skills, values, and dispositions. The second is the domain of *socialisation*, which is concerned with the ways in which, through education, we have become part of existing traditions and ways of doing and being. The third is the domain of *subjectification*, which is concerned with the interest of education in the subjectivity of those we educate. It has to do with emancipation and freedom and with the responsibility that comes with freedom.

Education, so argues Biesta, is not just about the reproduction of what we already know or of what already exists but is genuinely interested in the ways in which new beginnings and new beginners can come into the world, not just how we can get the world into our learners. And this is the crucial point: if we view education – as opposed to training – as a way of creating new knowledge, not just of 'passing on' existing knowledge, and as a means of developing people who will, in turn, create new things, then we must encourage learners' wider personal development and allow for choice and creativity, difference and divergence. Education cannot conform; it cannot inflexibly follow a prescription if it is to focus on how we help our learners to engage with, and thus come into, the world.

In short, education is about learning the best that has been thought and said – Gradgrind's "nothing but facts" – and then learning how to apply those facts in a range of different contexts and making connections between them. But it is also concerned with the interaction between human beings; it is about helping learners to change, to become something new and different and to see and interact with the world in new and different ways.

In an SSAT pamphlet on *Principled Curriculum*,[3] Dylan Wiliam set out four purposes of education as follows:

1. Personal empowerment: To allow young people to take greater control of their own lives.

2. Cultural transmission: To pass on from one generation to the next the best that has been thought and known in the world.

3. Preparation for citizenship: To prepare young people to make informed decisions about their participation in democratic society.

4. Preparation for work: To help young people become more productive and achieve economic prosperity.

These four might usefully define our programme of personal development.

A further thought: an effective programme of personal development provides opportunities for learners to acquire academic knowledge (a curriculum of the **head**), practical skills and talents, including in the arts (a curriculum of the **hand**), and personal skills and attributes (a curriculum of the **heart**).

Peter Hyman, in an article entitled *Success in the 21st Century*,[4] defined the head, hand, and heart as follows:

Head: An academic education [that] gives people in-depth knowledge of key concepts and ways of thinking in science, maths and design, as well as history and culture. This knowledge should be empowering knowledge . . . but importantly it should be shaped and applied to the needs of the present and future.

Hand: A can-do education that nurtures creativity and problem-solving, that gives young people the chance to respond to client briefs, to understand design thinking, to apply knowledge and conceptual understanding to new situations – to be able to make and do and produce work through craftsmanship that is of genuine value beyond the classroom.

Heart: A character education that provides the experiences and situations from which young people can develop a set of ethical underpinnings, well-honed character traits of resilience, kindness and tolerance, and a subtle, open mind.

Hyman added that

> Variety, depth, scholarship and real-world learning are all important components of a 21st century education that balances head, heart and hand. There is a value in short mastery lessons on grammar. A value, too, in the scholarship of studying Shakespeare, Chaucer or medieval England in depth – not for their relevance but for their own sake. But there is also a growing case for connecting learning to the real world. Giving students real experiences and placements that develop the six attributes [of] eloquence, grit, spark, professionalism, expertise, craftsmanship.

The measure of success for personal development

In sum, an effective programme of personal development can be measured by the extent to which it prepares all learners in school for their next steps. Do learners make good progress through the curriculum and go on to achieve positive destinations? Do learners leave school as well-rounded, cultured, inquisitive, caring, kind, resilient, knowledgeable human beings ready to make their own way in the world? Do we make the world a better place, one learner at a time?

To evaluate the extent to which learners are being prepared for the next stage of their lives, we might place emphasis on progression and destination data, understanding where learners go next, and whether this represents a positive step in the right direction and is ambitious and challenging.

Enrichment opportunities, as well as the development of oracy skills (perhaps through debating societies), might form part of this picture, too, demonstrating how seriously we take the holistic education of our learners. Enrichment is particularly important for disadvantaged learners who are not afforded the same opportunities outside school to develop their cultural capital and wider skills. The resultant skills gap is often what holds these learners back in the workplace and in life.

Although it is tempting to focus on how the taught curriculum (that which takes place in lessons) helps learners prepare for the next stage of their lives, we must not forget that learners are also informed by messages sent through the 'hidden' curriculum, those parts of the educational experience that occur in the spaces between lessons. In other words, what do the words and actions of all the adults in the school say to learners about what values and attitudes matter most in life and about how to behave as a citizen and employee?

We should also consider whether the skills that learners need to be prepared for the next stage of their lives are taught explicitly or implicitly, in isolation as 'transferable skills' or through a subject discipline as a domain-specific skill. For example, critical thinking is not a transferable skill because it is impossible to be critical about something on which you have little or no background knowledge. Learners must first acquire deep knowledge on a subject before they can be taught how to think critically about that subject. However, we may decide that some skills are indeed transferable because they are used in many subjects across the curriculum and in similar ways. Take, for example, structuring an argument, working in a team, giving feedback to a peer, internet research, note-taking, and so on.

A further point to note is the importance of information, advice, and guidance, including impartial careers guidance and guidance on which qualifications to study. If learners are not appropriately and expertly advised about the paths they can take, how can they be expected to take the right paths and be prepared for whatever awaits them around the next corner?

Finally, we need to consider what we do to help learners adjust to all the changes they face whilst in education. This includes the transition between schools as well as between the various phases, stages, and years of education.

Personal development and inclusion

Personal development is crucial for all learners, but arguably, it matters more to disadvantaged learners and learners with SEND because they are likely to arrive at school with gaps in their wider knowledge and skills and with fewer opportunities to experience the world.

Certainly, disadvantaged learners are more at risk of low self-efficacy because if you grow up in a family where adults did not do well at school, this will affect your own view of education and your belief in your ability to work hard and make progress. You're also more likely to witness your family feeling powerless in the face of adversity. Your parents' jobs are less likely to offer autonomy, and their purchasing power will be limited. In short, your family's lives will be driven by other people's decisions.

Low self-efficacy is cyclical: it contributes to lower attainment and is a result of lower attainment. The development of learners' non-cognitive and metacognitive skills – such as concentration and control and self-awareness and reflection – is as important as developing their cognitive skills.

So, what can we do to help learners develop self-efficacy? Here are some practical tips:

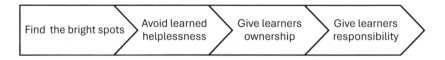

Figure 10.1 Tips for developing self-efficacy

1. Find the bright spots

Albert Einstein reportedly said that, "Everybody is a genius, but if you judge a fish by its ability to climb a tree, it will spend its whole life believing it is stupid". Traditional systems of assessment tend to recognise a narrow field of achievement, and some learners go through school thinking they're dumb. To counter this, we should try to identify some aspect of school life where each learner *is* excelling – or at least enjoying themselves and performing well – and then reward them for it. We should consider having awards for 'most improved' or 'best effort', and for 'pursuing a personal interest', as well as for what learners are doing outside of school.

Every learner can be outstanding at something – we just need to find the bright spots. This is, in part, about focusing on learners' effort and hard work not – or at least not solely – on their attainment. Everyone can try hard, and praising effort is a great leveller and a great way to motivate learners to work even harder. Likewise, praising learners for their metacognition – how self-aware they are, how they manage their emotions, how they monitor their progress, how they self-reflect, how independent they are, etc. – is another way to find the bright spots and to focus learners on the traits and dispositions that will help them to make future progress. Indeed, praising effort and metacognition go hand-in-hand because, that way, we recognise the strategies that underpin sustained effort.

2. Avoid learned helplessness

Self-efficacy is – by definition – about learners taking control. Often, though, disadvantaged learners and learners with SEND are over-supported to the point that they develop learned helplessness.

The SEND Code of Practice (2015) states that "with high aspirations, and the right support, the vast majority of children and young people can go on to achieve successful long-term outcomes in adult life". To achieve this aim, all professionals working with families should look to "enable children and young people to make choices for themselves from an early age".

The aim of any form of additional intervention and support is for the scaffolding to fall away gradually so that learners can become increasingly independent. Sometimes, as an unintended consequence of such support, learners develop learned helplessness, which is a state that occurs when a person comes to believe that they are unable to control or change a situation, so they do not try – even when opportunities for change become available.

Cognitively, learned helplessness occurs when a teacher, teaching assistant, or peer completes work for a learner or provides detailed cues or prompts, thus robbing the learner of the opportunity to complete the task for themselves. Put simply: If they do not think for themselves, they will not learn for themselves. Until a learner has been challenged to think through a task from start to finish, thus engaging in the decision-making processes, they will not be able to do so at a later time or in different circumstances, such as in a test.

Though some learners undoubtedly need additional or different types of support from time to time, they must also be afforded the chance to complete tasks independently, or else they will never close the gap between themselves and their peers. Their disadvantage will become their destiny.

The EEF, based on the work of Bosanquet, Radford, and Webster (2016),[5] propose a hierarchy of activities that promote learners' autonomy and independence. They suggest that, when supporting learners, we should start with self-scaffolding, which involves the greatest level of learner independence, then move on to prompting if learners require more help, followed by clueing, modelling, and then correcting.

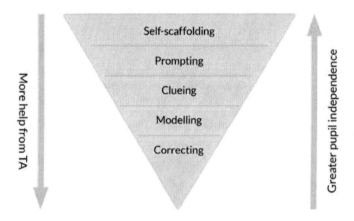

Figure 10.2 Avoiding learned helplessness

A. Self-scaffolding: In other words, observe and give learners time for processing and thinking.

Self-scaffolders can plan how to approach a task, problem-solve as they go, and review how they approached a task.

B. Prompting: In other words, provide prompts when learners are unable to self-scaffold.

Prompts encourage learners to draw on their own knowledge but refrain from specifying a strategy. The aim is to nudge learners into deploying a self-scaffolding technique. For example: 'What do you need to do first?'; 'What's your plan?'; 'You can do this!'

C. Clueing: In other words, provide a hint because learners often know the strategies or knowledge required to solve a problem but find it difficult to call them to mind.

Clues worded as questions provide a hint in the right direction. The answer must contain a key piece of information to help learners work out how to move forward. Always start with a small clue.

D. Modelling: In other words, model a step, then ask learners to repeat it.

Prompts and clues can be ineffective when learners encounter a task that requires a new skill or strategy. Here, teachers, as confident and competent experts, can model while learners actively watch and listen. Learners should then try the same step for themselves immediately afterwards.

E. Correcting: In other words, provide answers and require no independent thinking.

Occasionally, it is appropriate to do this; however, we should always aim instead to model and encourage learners to apply new skills or knowledge first.

3. Give learners ownership

Agency is important. Choice matters. One way to give learners greater control of their learning is to encourage them to set their own goals or to involve them in target-setting. One popular strategy in schools is to rank tasks by level of challenge and give learners a choice over which task they undertake. Although the levels of challenge may take the form of a Nando's-style chili pepper rating, they are often underpinned by the three zones influenced by Vygotsky and Bjork: the comfort zone, the struggle zone, and the panic zone. When using such a strategy, caution is needed to ensure some learners don't opt for the easy choice. We need to teach them that, tempting as it might be to stay within our comfort zone, this is not where we learn new things. Equally, we are not likely to learn when in the panic zone because this is where the neocortex gives way to the limbic system. The struggle zone is where learning takes place.

As well as setting their own goals and selecting task difficulty, learners can take control by engaging in self- and peer-assessment. For this to work, we need to ensure that learners know what they're assessing and how to give feedback. This requires clear success criteria and teacher modelling.

This talks about one of the key strategies of formative assessment:[6] Activating learners as instructional resources for each other. However, such strategies come with health warnings. Firstly, we need to help learners develop the necessary skills and knowledge to be able to assess and give feedback. Secondly, we need to provide learners with time in lessons to process, reflect upon, and respond to peer feedback.

This process of self-monitoring, self-assessing, and self-adjusting can be aided if we:

- Allocate five minutes in the middle and at the end of a lesson to consider 'What have we found out? What remains unresolved or unanswered?'

- Ask learners to attach a self-assessment form to every formal piece of work they hand in.

- Include a one-minute essay at the end of an instruction-based lesson in which learners summarise the two or three main points and the questions that remain for them (and, thus, next time, for the teacher).

- Ask learners to attach a note to any formal piece of work in which they are honest about what they do and do not understand.

- Teach learners to evaluate work in the same way that teachers do so that learners become more accurate as peer reviewers and self-assessors and more inclined to 'think like teachers' in their work.

- Start lessons with a survey of the most burning questions learners may have. Then, as part of the final plenary, judge how well the questions were addressed, which ones remain, and what new ones emerged.

- Leave the second half of a unit deliberately 'open' to allow learners to frame and pursue the inquiry (rather than be directed by the teacher) based on the key questions that remain and clues that emerge at the end of the first half.

- Get learners to develop a self-profile of their strengths and weaknesses as learners at the start of the year, whereby they consider how they learn best, what strategies work well for them, what type of learning is most difficult, and what they wish to improve upon. Then, structure periodic opportunities for pupils to monitor their efforts and reflect on their struggles, successes, and possible edits to their own profiles.

Another simple method to help learners take ownership of their own learning is to give each learner a laminated card, green on one side and red on the other. At the start of the lesson, the card is placed on the learner's desk with the green side facing upwards. Once the teacher has given an explanation, if the learner doesn't understand it, they flip the card over to red. As soon as one learner flips the card to red, the teacher selects a learner who is still showing green, and that learner answers a question that the learner who's showing red wants to ask. This approach means learners are constantly required to think about whether they understand or not, which is an example of metacognition.

4. Give learners responsibility

Learners can take responsibility, not just for their own learning, but for the success of their school. Many schools run student councils or junior leadership teams. Many have class representatives and peer mentor schemes. And many have head boys and girls. What these student leaders do with their positions is vital. They must not be titles alone but rather active roles in the school improvement process. They must have a real voice and represent learners' views during decision-making. For example, student leaders could take control of parents' consultation evenings, send invitations to parents, greet visitors, provide refreshments, give short talks, and display work. Likewise, student leaders could present at open evenings and events. Student leaders could also have a seat at the table during some senior leadership meetings and governing body meetings, presenting their own papers. School council members could play a part in staff recruitment by interviewing candidates.

Not only is this a great way to help disenfranchised learners feel that they belong and have a part to play in school, but it also helps bolster disadvantaged learners' CVs and gives them vital leadership skills that help prepare them for future success.

Notes

1 Dickens, C. (1854). *Hard times*. Household Words.
2 Biesta, G. (2015). What is education for? On good education, teacher judgement, and educational professionalism. *European Journal of Education*, *50*(1), 75–87. https://doi.org/10.1111/ejed.12109

3 Wiliam, D. (2013). *Principled curriculum design*. SSAT. https://webcontent.ssatuk.co.uk/wp-content/uploads/2023/12/05151905/SSAT-Redesigning-Schooling-03-Principled-curriculum-design.pdf

4 Hymen, P. (2017). *Success in the 21st century: The education of head, heart and hand*. IPPR. https://ippr-org.files.svdcdn.com/production/Downloads/success-in-the-21st-century-may2017.pdf

5 Bosanquet, P., Radford, J., & Webster, R. (2016). *The teaching assistant's guide to effective interaction: How to maximise your practice*. Routledge.

6 Wiliam, D., & Thompson, M. (2007). Integrating assessment with instruction: What will it take to make it work? In C. A. Dwyer (Ed.), *The future of assessment: Shaping teaching and learning* (pp. 53–82). Lawrence Erlbaum Associates.

Behaviours for future success

We're still exploring the fifth aspect of creating a culture of good behaviours – a programme of personal development to foster learners' independence. So far, we've looked at the purpose of education, arguing that our job in school is to prepare learners for the next stage of their lives. We've examined some measures of success for our programme of personal development and explored the role of personal development in achieving inclusion. Now we'll look at the logistics: how can we deliver a programme of personal development to aid us in our quest to build equity in the education system and ensure greater inclusion in our schools?

We will explore the following:

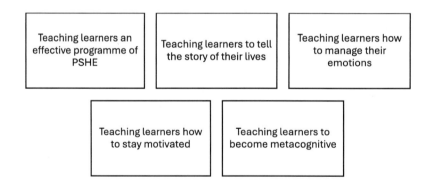

Figure 11.1 Elements of the personal development programme

Teaching learners an effective programme of PSHE

A learner's personal development should pervade school life, weaving through the curriculum and extra-curricular provision, as well as in the interactions that take place outside the classroom. But, one of the primary sources of teaching personal development is through personal, social, health, and economic education or PSHE.

Twenty years ago, I became a PSHE coordinator and attempted to change teachers' and learners' attitudes to that much-maligned subject. My initial task was to rebrand the discipline and after much consultation with staff, I settled on *Life Skills*. Next, I conducted an audit of the curriculum to ensure that it was up-to-date and relevant and that each year of study built upon the previous.

I debated whether PSHE should be taught by form tutors or specialist teachers and found a happy compromise: PSHE would be taught by pastoral teams, but we would develop specialist teachers within each team.

I developed a curriculum comprising six common modules per year and produced curriculum plans and resources, including culturally relevant and interactive resources, and tailored these to the school context. I consulted with tutors to decide who had the most relevant skills and knowledge to teach each module so that not only did staff get to teach a topic about which they were knowledgeable, but they also got to teach one module repeated six times a year rather than six different modules.

Next, I made the decision not to compel anyone to teach relationships and sex education (RSE) but to rely on willing volunteers, as this, I knew, was uncomfortable for some members of staff. The willing volunteers then worked together on planning, with expert advice from external agencies.

Finally, I set up two half-termly meetings: one was for each pastoral team so they could liaise on the teaching of their year group and ensure a smooth transition as learners moved from one module to the next, and the second was for all the teachers of a particular module so they could ensure that what was taught in one year was developed the next.

Twenty years later, I still believe in the power of PSHE. PSHE is a vital part of the school curriculum and an essential component of a well-rounded education. It also makes a significant contribution to several other statutory responsibilities placed on schools, including the responsibility to promote learners' personal and economic wellbeing. The national curriculum also makes clear that every state-funded school in England has to offer a curriculum which promotes the spiritual, moral, cultural, mental, and physical development of learners and which prepares learners for the opportunities, responsibilities, and experiences of later life. PSHE is well-placed to fulfil both of these duties.

I would argue that an effective programme of PSHE is marked by the following characteristics:

- The quality of teaching is good because teachers are well-trained and are helped to develop expertise in teaching sensitive and, at times, controversial issues.

- RSE lessons are taught by teachers with specialist knowledge, and these lessons focus on how learners can stay safe.

- PSHE lessons help learners develop self-esteem, resilience, and communication skills such as advocacy, negotiation, and persuasion.

- PSHE coordinators are well-trained, regularly meet the team of teachers who teach PSHE, and observe PSHE lessons.

- PSHE is a priority for the headteacher and school leaders and features in school development plans and self-evaluation.

- The curriculum and the quality of teaching are constantly reviewed by teachers, learners, parents, and families to ensure it continues to meet needs.

In terms of what this looks like in practice, I would suggest that PSHE works best when . . .

- There is a detailed understanding of and support for PSHE by the headteacher and school leaders.

- School leaders and governors are kept regularly informed and involved in developments in PSHE.

- PSHE is timetabled when teachers and learners are most likely to engage in it.

- Timetabled PSHE lessons are complemented by regular off-timetable days or events.

- PSHE is taught by teachers with specialist knowledge and an interest in the topic they deliver.

- PSHE is treated on a par with other subjects, including in how it is planned, taught, and assessed.

- Data about learner performance in PSHE is collated and used to inform planning and teaching, as well as reported to parents.

- PSHE forms part of whole-school systems of self-evaluation and improvement planning, as well as quality assurance, such as learning walks and work scrutiny.

- There is access to appropriate staff training.

- PSHE is included in the agenda of regular staff, school leadership, and governor meetings.

- There is regular involvement of the community and external agencies in the development and delivery of PSHE.

- The PSHE curriculum is joined-up and progressive and contains up-to-date and relevant materials.

Teaching learners how to tell the story of their lives

One of the aims of a successful PSHE programme is to help learners tell a positive story about their lives and futures. Indeed, this is something I explored in my last book, *The Stories We Tell*.[1]

I argued that stories can help learners understand themselves and their place in the world. A learner's life story influences their daily experience. It is their unique take on the 'good' and 'bad' experiences they've had, the choices they've made, and the significance of the people they've met. However, learners are unreliable writers of their own stories, so teaching learners about story can improve their self-perception *and* help them develop a habit of questioning their own perceptions, beliefs, and ways of thinking. Story can also help learners improve their perception of other people because listening to stories from those with different experiences to our own enables us to develop empathy.

Coming from a disadvantaged background or having additional and different needs can make learners feel that they don't belong in school. Limited life experiences, such as eating

Behaviours for future success **113**

in a restaurant, going on a foreign holiday, visiting the countryside, going to a museum or art gallery, and so on, can lead to a belief that they don't have a place in the world of education. To counter this, learners need to know that they have the power to make their story the best possible version of themselves. This doesn't mean creating a fake story in which they project themselves in a way that makes others like them more or which denies their roots – that's the *conditioned self*. Rather, it's about creating a story that makes them happy and content, one where they live by their values – this is the *authentic self*. Thus, as part of our programme of personal development, and perhaps through PSHE, we need to help learners tell the story of their authentic selves and be proud of who they are and where they come from, as well as unafraid to encounter new people and places, make new memories, and tell new stories.

Another aspect of preparing learners for future success through story and storytelling that I explored in *The Stories We Tell* is to equip them with an armoury of life skills.

A decade or so ago, when I was a headteacher, I interviewed 50 learners in Years 11 and 13 who had achieved high grades in their GCSE and A level exams. I discovered a series of apparent coincidences:

- All the learners I interviewed had an attendance of more than 95%; 90% of them had a perfect attendance record.

- All the learners I interviewed told me they used their planners regularly and considered themselves to be well organised. As a result, they all completed their homework on time and without fail.

- All the learners I interviewed told me they always asked for help from their teachers when they got stuck. They didn't regard doing so as a sign of weakness but rather a sign of strength. Admitting they didn't know something and asking questions meant they learned something new and increased their intelligence.

- Most of the learners I interviewed were involved in clubs, sports, or hobbies at lunchtime, after school, and/or at weekends. Though not all were sporting, they did all have get-up-and-go attitudes. They didn't spend every evening and weekend watching television or glued to their mobile phones. They were sociable and, to unwind, they read books. Lots of books. In fact, the school library confirmed that my cohort of 50 high achievers were among the biggest borrowers in school.

- All the learners I interviewed believed that doing well in school would increase their chances of getting higher-paid and more interesting jobs later in life. Many of them had a clear idea about the kind of job they wanted to do and knew what was needed to get it. They had researched the entry requirements and had then mapped out the necessary school, college, and/or university paths. They had connected what they were doing in school with achieving their future ambitions. School work and good exam results had a purpose; they were means to an important end. In other words, they had written the story of their own futures – they had a clear narrative that gave purpose to their lives and learning.

But were these coincidences, or was it a simple case of cause and effect: *because* these learners shared these traits, they went on to succeed? I believe it was the latter: it was because these learners had attended school, were well organised, completed work on time, and had an end goal in mind that they had achieved excellent grades in their final exams. The cause was diligent study and determination – writing their own story; the effect was high achievement.

We might conclude that the recipe for success is:

Figure 11.2 Four ingredients in the recipe for success

We would be wise to place these success criteria at the heart of our programme of personal development. For example, we could have a study skills module in PSHE which teaches learners how to be well-organised and engage in meaningful self-study. Here are some suggested skills we might teach:

Figure 11.3 Five study skills to explicitly teach

Self-quizzing

Self-quizzing is about retrieving knowledge and skills from memory and is far more effective than simply re-reading. When learners read a text or study notes, we might encourage them to pause periodically to ask themselves questions – without looking at the text – such as:

- What are the key ideas?
- What terms or ideas are new to me? How would I define them?
- How do the ideas in this text relate to what I already know?

Elaboration

Elaboration is the process of finding additional layers of meaning in new material. It involves relating new material to what learners already know, explaining it to somebody else, or explaining how it relates to the wider world.

Generation

Generation is when learners attempt to answer a question or solve a problem before being shown the answer or the solution. The act of filling in a missing word (a cloze test) leads to a stronger memory of the text than simply reading it. Before reading new texts in class, we might ask learners to explain the key ideas they expect to find and how they expect these ideas will relate to their prior knowledge.

Reflection

Reflection involves taking a moment to review what has been learned. Learners might ask themselves questions such as:

- What went well? What could have gone better?
- What other knowledge or experience does it remind me of?
- What might I need to learn to achieve better mastery?
- What strategies could I use next time to get better results?

Calibration

Calibration is achieved when learners adjust their judgement to reflect reality – in other words, they become certain that their sense of what they know and can do is accurate. Often, when we revise information, we look at a question and convince ourselves that we know the answer and then move on to the next question without trying to actually answer the previous one. But if we do not write down an answer, we may create the illusion of knowing when, in fact, we would find it difficult to give a response. We, therefore, need to teach learners to remove the illusion of knowing and answering all the questions, even if they think they know the answer and that it is too easy.

Here are some other study skills we might teach our learners in PSHE:

1. How to formulate helpful questions while reading a text.

2. How to find terms they can't recall or don't know while reading a text – then learn them.

3. How to copy key terms from a text – and their definitions – into a notebook.

4. How to take regular practice tests.

5. How to reorganise class material into a study guide.

116 Why School Doesn't Work for Every Child

6. How to copy out key concepts and regularly test themselves on them.

7. How to space out revision and practice activities.

Teaching learners how to manage their emotions

Another important life skill we might embed in the PSHE curriculum is managing emotions.

Earlier in this book, I mentioned the fight-or-flight response. There is a constant battle in the human brain between, in the red corner, the frontal cortex, and, in the blue corner, the limbic system. The frontal cortex is the rational side; the limbic system is irrational. The limbic system has been called 'the chimp' (by, for example, Professor Steve Peters in his book *The Chimp Paradox*)[2] because it is the primitive part of our brain and often tries to control our actions with pure, naked instincts. It asks, 'How do I feel?' rather than 'What do I think?' It seeks an emotional fight or flight response to conflict. The frontal cortex, meanwhile, is the rational side, which is concerned with thoughts rather than feelings. It asks, 'What is logical?'

Unfortunately, the limbic system – because it works on instinct – is faster to act than the frontal cortex, which takes time to consider what is rational under the circumstances and seeks to place events in context. This is why there is a constant war being waged in our heads. Our frontal cortex is always trying to wrest back control from the limbic system. Professor Daniel Kahneman[3] calls the limbic system System A and the frontal cortex System B, arguing – including in the title of his book – that there is a conflict between these systems, which can be summarised as *Thinking, Fast and Slow*.

Whenever we face conflict, our frontal cortex and our limbic system do battle in this way. The chimp goes into fight or flight mode and makes us emotional and irrational. It gets our blood pumping, our heart racing, and our dander up. But this is the worst possible way to respond to conflict. It's important, therefore, to acknowledge the chimp's existence and be mindful of how it's trying to shape our response. And then, we need to put the chimp back in its cage and allow our frontal cortex to take control and provide a logical, rational response that stands up to scrutiny.

One way to help learners manage their emotions is to encourage them to start with the self – to soul-search in order to become more self-aware. Developing a sense of emotional intelligence is one way to do this. Daniel Goleman developed a three-step model of emotional intelligence:

1. Know yourself (what he called self-mastery)

2. Know others (what he called social radar)

3. Control your response

Emotional intelligence is commonly defined as the ability to understand ourselves and other people. This comprises the ability to manage and express our emotions and respond to other people's emotions in ways that are productive. In his book *Emotional Intelligence*,[4] Goleman posited five skill domains that might also feature as part of our programme of personal development:

1. Self-awareness

2. Managing feelings

3. Motivation

4. Empathy

5. Social skills

Emotional intelligence allows us to model the sorts of behavioural responses we expect to see from others. If we don't model the desired behaviours, then we cannot expect our learners to mirror them and to behave more appropriately towards us and each other. We also need learners to be more aware of their own ongoing emotional state and conduct a realistic assessment of their own strengths and weaknesses. We need learners to be aware of the emotional state of those around them, too, and to be able to deploy appropriate and measured responses.

To be confident of accurately self-assessing, we need to teach learners how to become aware of their strengths and weaknesses, how to be reflective, and how to learn from their experiences. We need learners to be open to candid feedback, to new perspectives, and to continuous learning and self-development.

To be self-confident, learners need to be able to present themselves with self-assurance, showing conviction of purpose and belief. This requires the explicit teaching of oracy skills, such as constructing an argument and debating different sides.

To be emotionally aware, learners need to know which emotions they are feeling and why, recognise the links between their feelings and what they think, do, and say, recognise how their feelings affect their performance, and never lose sight of their values and goals.

Teaching learners how to stay motivated

Another important aspect of personal development is helping learners to stay motivated to learn. Broadly speaking, there are two types of motivation that matter most to our learners' personal development: intrinsic and extrinsic.

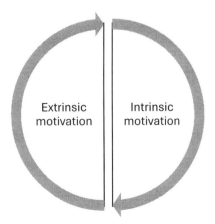

Figure 11.4 Types of motivation

Intrinsic motivation is the self-desire to seek out new things and new challenges, to gain new knowledge. Often, intrinsic motivation is driven by an inherent interest or enjoyment in the task itself and exists within an individual rather than relying on external pressures or necessity. Put simply, it's the desire to do something even though there is no reward except a sense of accomplishment at achieving that thing. Intrinsic motivation is a natural motivational tendency and is a critical element in cognitive, social, and physical development.

Learners who are intrinsically motivated are more likely to engage in a task willingly as well as work to improve their skills, which – in turn – increases their capabilities. Learners are likely to be intrinsically motivated if they develop:

1. *Autonomy* by attributing their educational results to factors under their own control.

2. *Self-efficacy* by believing in their own ability to succeed in specific situations or to accomplish a task.

3. *Mastery* by being genuinely interested in accomplishing something to a high level of proficiency, knowledge, and skill, not just in achieving good grades.

Extrinsic motivation, meanwhile, refers to the performance of an activity to attain a desired outcome. Extrinsic motivation comes from influences outside an individual's control, a rationale, a necessity, or a need. Common forms of extrinsic motivation are rewards (for example, money or prizes) or – conversely – the threat of punishment.

We can provide learners with a rationale for learning by sharing the 'big picture' with them. In other words, we can continually explain how their learning fits into a topic, unit, or subject discipline, as well as their careers, and to success in work and life. For example, we can explain how today's lesson connects with yesterday's lesson and how the learning will be extended or consolidated in tomorrow's lesson. We can explain how this learning will become useful in later life, too, and we can connect the learning in one subject with the learning in other subjects, making explicit the transferability of knowledge and skills and the interconnectedness of skills in everyday life.

This is not to suggest that learners will possess either intrinsic or extrinsic motivation. Rather, it is desirable for learners to possess or develop both. Learners should both *want* and *need* to learn. However, it is more likely that disadvantaged learners and learners with SEND will lack the *want* to learn and so instilling in them the *need* to learn becomes even more important. As such, here are two practical suggestions for building learners' motivation:

1. Engender a culture of excellence in the classroom

The first step towards motivating learners to produce high-quality work is to set tasks which inspire and challenge them and which are predicated on the idea that every learner will succeed, not just finish the task but produce work which represents personal excellence.

The most effective tasks offer learners an opportunity to engage in genuine research, not just that invented for the classroom. What's more, a learner's finished product needs a real audience. This means there is a genuine reason to do the work well, not just because the teacher wants it that way. Not every piece of work can be of genuine importance, of course, but every piece of work can be displayed, presented, appreciated, and judged by people outside the classroom.

Classwork also works best when it is structured in such a way as to make it difficult for learners to fall too far behind or fail. Tasks also work best when they are broken into a set of clear components so that learners must progress through checkpoints to ensure they are keeping up. Good tasks have in-built flexibility to allow for learners with differing starting points and with different needs.

Classwork works best when it has in-built rubrics, or checklists, if you like, which make clear what is expected of each learner at each stage of development. In other words, the rubric spells out exactly what components are required in the assignment, what the timeline for completion is, and on what qualities and dimensions the work will be judged. However, it is not enough simply to make a list, a rubric, of what makes a good finished product, be that an essay or a science experiment. It is not enough to read a great piece of literature and analyse the writing or to look at the work of a great scientist. If we want learners to write a strong essay or design a strong experiment, we need to show them what a great essay or experiment looks like. We need to admire models, find inspiration in them, and analyse their strengths and weaknesses. In short, we need to work out what makes them strong.

2. Make learning meaningful

Learners are motivated to learn when they regard classwork as personally meaningful and when learning fulfils an educational purpose. Classwork can be made personally meaningful if we begin by triggering learners' curiosity. In other words, at the start of the first lesson on a new topic, we could use a 'hook' to engage our learners' interest and initiate questioning. A hook can be anything: an anecdote, a video, a lively discussion, a guest speaker, a story, a field trip, or a text.

Many learners find schoolwork meaningless because they don't perceive a need to know what they're being taught. They are not motivated by their teacher's insistence that they should learn something because they'll need it later in life, for the next module on the course, or because it might be in the exam. With a compelling task, however, the reason for the learning becomes clear: learners need to know this in order to meet the challenge they've just accepted.

Classwork can also be made personally meaningful to learners if we pose a big question that captures the heart of a topic in clear, compelling language and gives learners a sense of purpose and challenge. A big question should be provocative, open, and complex. The question can be abstract or concrete, or it can be focused on solving a problem. Without a big question, learners may not understand why they are undertaking a task. They may know that the series of activities they are engaged in are in some way connected but may not be clear as to how or why.

Classwork can be made personally meaningful to learners if they are given some choice about how to conduct the work and present their findings. Indeed, the more choice, the better. Where choice is limited, learners can select what topic to study within a general big question or choose how to design, create, and present their findings.

Classwork can fulfil an educational purpose if it provides opportunities to build metacognition and character skills such as collaboration, communication, and critical thinking, which will serve learners well in the workplace as in life.

Classwork can fulfil an educational purpose if it makes learning meaningful by emphasising the need to create high-quality products and performances through the formal use of feedback and drafting. Learners need to learn that most people's first attempts don't result in high quality. Instead, frequent revision is a feature of real-world work. In addition to providing direct feedback, we can coach learners in using rubrics and other sets of assessment criteria for learners to critique each other's work.

Teaching learners how to be metacognitive

Once learners are motivated to learn, we need to help them manage the learning process. Metacognition describes the processes involved when learners plan, monitor, evaluate, and make changes to their own learning behaviours. Metacognition is often considered to have two dimensions:

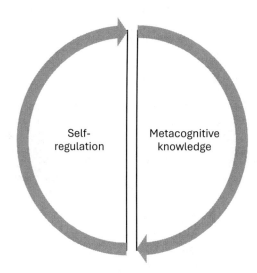

Figure 11.5 The two dimensions of metacognition

Metacognitive knowledge refers to what learners *know* about learning. This includes:

- The learner's knowledge of their own cognitive abilities (e.g., 'I have trouble remembering key dates in this period of history')

- The learner's knowledge of particular tasks (e.g., 'The politics in this period of history are complex')

- The learner's knowledge of the different strategies that are available to them and when they are appropriate to the task (e.g., 'If I create a timeline first, it will help me to understand this period of history').

Self-regulation, meanwhile, refers to what learners *do* about learning. It describes how they monitor and control their cognitive processes. For example, a learner might realise that a particular strategy is not yielding the results they expected, so they decide to try a different strategy. Put another way, self-regulated learners are aware of their strengths and weaknesses and can motivate themselves to engage in and improve their learning.

In practice, metacognition and self-regulation might take the following form:

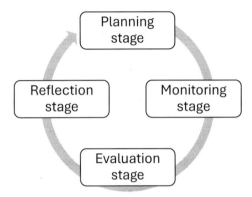

Figure 11.6 The metacognitive cycle

The planning stage:

During the planning stage, learners think about the goal the teacher has set and consider how they will approach the task and what strategies they will use. At this stage, it is helpful for learners to ask themselves:

- 'What am I being asked to do?'
- 'Which strategies will I use?'
- 'Are there any strategies that I have used before that might be useful?'

The monitoring stage:

During the monitoring stage, learners implement their plan and monitor the progress they are making towards their learning goal. Learners might decide to make changes to the strategies they are using if these are not working. As learners work through the task, it is helpful to ask themselves:

- 'Is the strategy that I am using working?'
- 'Do I need to try something different?'

The evaluation stage:

During the evaluation stage, learners determine how successful the strategy they've used has been in terms of helping them achieve their learning goal. To promote evaluation, it is helpful for learners to ask themselves:

- 'How well did I do?'

- 'What didn't go well?' 'What could I do differently next time?'

- 'What went well?' 'What other types of problem can I use this strategy for?'

The reflection stage:

Reflection is an integral part of the whole process. Encouraging learners to self-question throughout the process is therefore crucial.

What does personal development look like?

The schools' inspectorate in England, Ofsted, has a judgement area called Personal Development, which is instructive in terms of defining some of the success criteria for an effective programme of personal development. Ofsted said[5] that personal development is about . . .

- Developing learners as responsible, respectful, and active citizens who are able to play their part and become actively involved in public life as adults.

- Developing and deepening learners' understanding of human values such as democracy, individual liberty, the rule of law, and mutual respect and tolerance.

- Promoting equality of opportunity so that all learners can thrive together, understanding that difference is a positive, not a negative, and that individual characteristics make people unique.

- Promoting an inclusive environment that meets the needs of all learners, irrespective of age, disability, gender reassignment, race, religion or belief, or sex or sexual orientation.

- Developing learners' character so they are motivated and can reflect wisely, learn eagerly, behave with integrity, and cooperate consistently well with others.

- Developing learners' confidence, resilience, and knowledge so that they can keep themselves mentally healthy.

- Enabling learners to recognise online and offline risks to their well-being, including risks from criminal and sexual exploitation, domestic abuse, female genital mutilation, forced marriage, substance misuse, gang activity, radicalisation and extremism – and making them aware of the support available to them.

- Enabling learners to recognise the dangers of inappropriate use of mobile technology and social media.

- Developing learners' understanding of how to keep physically healthy, eat healthily, and maintain an active lifestyle, including giving ample opportunities for learners to be active during the school day and through extra-curricular activities.

- Developing learners' age-appropriate understanding of healthy relationships through appropriate relationship and sex education.

- Providing an effective careers programme that offers learners unbiased careers advice, the experience of work, and contact with employers, and that encourages learners to make good choices and understand what they need to do to reach and succeed in the careers to which they aspire.

- Supporting learners' readiness for the next phase of their education, training, or employment so that they are equipped to make the transition successfully.

Notes

1 Bromley, M. (2024). *The stories we tell: How to use story and storytelling to improve teaching and school leadership*. Routledge.
2 Peters, S. (2012). *The chimp paradox*. Vermilion.
3 Kahneman, D. (2011). *Thinking fast and slow*. Penguin.
4 Goleman, D. (1995). *Emotional intelligence: Why it can matter more than IQ*. Bloomsbury.
5 I have taken the liberty of amending this list to suit an international audience and better reflect the focus of this chapter; the original list can be found at https://www.gov.uk/government/publications/school-inspection-handbook-eif/school-inspection-handbook-for-september-2023#evaluating-personal-development

PART III
C is for community

12 Community and families first

Parental engagement

As I said earlier, it takes a village to raise a child and a whole community to educate one. Schools are not islands operating in isolation. Rather, they are a part of their community – an integral part, but a part nonetheless – and live to serve that community. Indeed, when I was a headteacher, I used to say that the school I led was not *my* school but that I was its custodian, looking after it on behalf of the community.

Parental engagement is, therefore, key to building more equity in education and creating more inclusive schools.

By way of a starting point, here are four cornerstones of effective parental engagement:

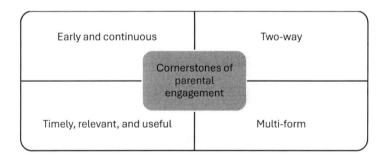

Figure 12.1 Cornerstones of effective parental engagement

1. **Parental engagement needs to start early and continue throughout a learner's journey through school.** The parents of children moving from primary to secondary won't want to receive information halfway through the summer holiday, at which point it will be deemed too late. Schools need to engage with parents early and clearly set out their expectations and requirements.

2. **Parental engagement needs to be a two-way process.** As well as the school staying in touch with parents, parents also need a means of staying connected with the school. One

way to do this is to create a frequently asked questions page, as well as a Q&A facility and a parents' forum on the school's website. This will need to be monitored carefully, of course, or perhaps have comments vetted by a gatekeeper before they are made live. For this to be viewed as worthwhile, the school will also need to communicate its response to parental comments and suggestions, perhaps through a 'You Said, We Did' page.

3. **Parental engagement needs to be appropriately timed, relevant, and useful.** One way to do this is to use the experience and expertise of learners and their parents. For example, the parents of current Year 7 learners will be able to share their thoughts on what information they needed when they went through the transition process with their child not so long ago, as well as when they needed it most. Meanwhile, current Year 7 learners will be able to offer their advice about how to prepare for secondary school – for example, by providing a reading list for the summer and sharing their tips on how to get ready for the first day of school.

4. **Parental engagement should take many forms and embrace new and emerging technologies.** The use of digital technologies such as email, texting, websites, videos, webinars, electronic portfolios, and online assessment and reporting tools can make communication between parents and teachers more timely, efficient, productive, and satisfying.

Of course, doing all of this well takes time, so it is important to balance the needs of parents and families with those of hard-working teachers. We don't want the unintended consequence of adding to teachers' workloads.

Whilst we want parents to work in partnership with us and for them to be involved in – not just informed about – our schools, we also need to remember that we are the gatekeepers for communication flow. Our colleagues need to be protected from over-zealous and needy parents who want to send hourly emails. Our colleagues also need to be shielded from angry and belligerent parents. Simple protocols and systems can mitigate these problems. For example, a parental engagement policy can solve a lot of these issues. Such a policy should do two things: firstly, set out clearly what parents and families can expect from the school and, secondly, set out what the school expects from parents and families.

We should always start with what parents and families can expect from the school. First and foremost, schools should show how they will make parents feel comfortable. It is far more likely that a parent of a disadvantaged learner will feel alienated by the experience of interacting with school staff. In our busy working lives, we can easily lose sight of this. Here are a few suggestions on how best to achieve this:

Parents and families can expect . . .

- To receive clear and timely communication about their child's progress.

- To attend parents' information events which offer high-quality interactions.

- To receive documentation that can be easily understood.

- The school to treat them and their child fairly and with dignity and respect.

- School rules to be clearly explained and enforced consistently.

In exchange, the school should encourage parents and families to . . .

- Be understanding, supportive, and communicative.
- Maintain a direct involvement in their child's education.
- Attend events or make alternative arrangements.
- Positively contribute to initiatives that support their child.
- Be aware of and support any home–school agreements.

A parental engagement policy should also outline how the school intends to communicate with parents and how it will consult with them on key decisions. It may be useful to start with a statement of intent such as: 'Our school, to be effective, must acknowledge, appreciate and respond to the views of parents. It needs to make informed decisions following consultation'.

Next, the school will need a clear strategy for communicating effectively and expediently with parents in myriad ways, including, though not exclusively, through parents' consultation evenings and other face-to-face events, through workshops and discussion forums, as well as parent–teacher associations or committees, through surveys and online reporting tools, and through newsletters, emails, text messages, and the school website.

Two-way communication involves parents hearing their voices reflected; they need to feel included and represented. We need more diverse voices in education to help disenfranchised parents feel that they belong and are welcome in school.

To be effective, parental communications need to be:

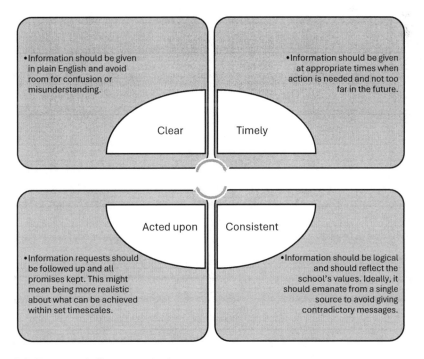

Figure 12.2 Features of effective parental communications

Parental communications can be improved by making a habit of positive praise – for example, weekly 'good news' telephone calls to parents by teachers and leaders can help to build rapport and establish a strong partnership. When a phone call from the school conveys good news – rather than always being about poor behaviour, attendance, or progress – the relationship between the school and home will improve.

However, particularly for new teachers, it can be difficult to make that first phone call to a parent. Preparing for the call makes it easier, and rehearsing the opening lines can alleviate some of the anxiety. Here are some guidelines to help teachers prepare for a phone call:

1. **Introduce yourself:** What is your name, what is your role in school and what is your relationship to the learner?

2. **Tell the parents what their child is studying in class:** What is the current topic, and how does it fit into the wider curriculum?

3. **Comment on their child's progress to date:** In what ways have they improved over time? What do you predict of their achievements this term or year?

4. **Comment on their child's behaviour and attitude to learning:** Are they attentive, keen, industrious, polite, helpful towards others, and so on?

5. **Inform them of their child's achievements:** Have they won any awards or received any house points?

6. **Inform them of their child's main strengths** or share an anecdote about their performance in class.

7. **Ensure the parent knows they can contact you** to discuss their child at any time in the future and remind them of the ways they can stay in touch with the school.

Additionally, here is a simple script that might work in reaching a hard-to-reach parent: 'Hello, is this [name of parent]? I'm calling from [name of school] with some good news about [name of learner]. Can I tell you about it?'

Engaging the parents of disadvantaged learners

In his book *Visible Learning* (2008),[1] John Hattie estimates that the effect of parental engagement is equivalent to two to three additional years of learning over a learner's school career. Arguably, the parents we need to engage the most are the parents of disadvantaged learners, yet these tend to be the hardest to reach.

In *Multiple disadvantage and KS4 attainment: evidence from LSYPE2* (Lessof et al., 2019),[2] after adjusting for the effect of the other types of disadvantage, the proportion of young people with parents showing less engagement who achieved good passes in English and maths was 24 percentage points lower than among learners whose parents were more engaged. Parental engagement was calculated based on learners' answers to three questions: how frequently parents discussed school reports with them, whether they attended parents' evenings, and how much parents talked with them about their future plans for studying.

We know there's a correlation between socio-economic disadvantage and levels of parental engagement. For example, a study by Marmot et al. (2020)[3] shows that children from higher-income families spend 30% more time on home learning than those from poorer families. This doesn't mean that every disadvantaged family will struggle to support their child's learning, however.

So, what can we do to reach the harder-to-reach parents of disadvantaged learners? Here are my six top tips:

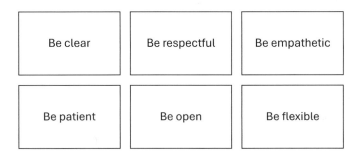

Figure 12.3 Six top tips for parental engagement

Be clear

Schools can be daunting places, and the way we communicate is important if we are to break down barriers – especially for those parents who had poor experiences at school when they were young or who fear institutions. It is, therefore, advisable to avoid not only confusing professional jargon but also formal language. For example, rather than offer 'parenting classes', we could run a 'Lads and Dads' session or a 'Family Friday'. Rather than have a 'Family Liaison Officer' or 'Community Worker', we could have a 'Parent Partner' or 'Family Link.'

As well as softening our language, we can offer enticements, such as 'food and fun!' Parents are more likely to attend a parent information evening if we advertise it as a 'pie and peas' night with a fun element such as a quiz before moving on to more educational matters, or a 'bun and book' event where parents have afternoon tea and read with their child. And even then, we need to think carefully about making such matters accessible.

First, we need to reduce the threat level. Many parents are scared of being asked to do something beyond their comfort zone or skill. So, rather than tasking parents with the job of educating their child by, for example, helping with homework, we could make clear that 'it's our job to teach your child – we just ask you talk to them about it'. Where we do want parents to play a more active role in their child's education, we should provide them with the tools they need, ideally in the form of 'one-side explainers', 'two-minute guides', or even short-form videos.

As a starting point, I'd suggest we offer explainers on:

- How to talk to your child about their homework
- How to read to your child and listen to them read
- How to establish healthy routines for mornings, homework, screentime, bedtime, etc.

Be respectful

We should always treat parents and families with dignity and respect and regard parents as equals who have a stake in our school. We should try to make parents feel welcome in school. We should try to be visible at times when parents might visit school, such as on the morning and afternoon school runs, at lunchtime, and during events such as sports days, school plays, and after-school clubs. We should try to engage parents in conversation just as we do with their children, perhaps by asking about their weekends.

In practical terms, being respectful also means that we start with what *we* can do, not what we expect parents to do. We should ask parents what they need from us, then try to provide it, rather than put the onus on parents.

So, what can we do for parents? By way of a starter for ten, we could:

- Run a breakfast club

- Run a homework club

- Offer a uniform bank

- Support a food bank

- Host a community hub giving access to advice on housing and healthcare

- Offer adult education classes

- Run sessions to help with parenting

Parent support sessions could include advice on how to handle challenging behaviour, encourage good sleep hygiene, and help children stay safe online, and so on. The key is to ensure that such sessions are not patronising, working on the assumption that we know best and wish to dictate to parents how to bring up their children. Rather, we should frame such sessions as non-judgemental opportunities to share what we do and to listen to parents' suggestions in the hope the school and home can speak with one voice and adopt one approach because consistency breeds compliance.

Be empathetic

It's tempting to assume that parents of disadvantaged learners lack the parenting skills needed to support their child or that they simply don't care. But this is rarely the case. For example, if a parent doesn't attend a scheduled meeting or show up to a parents' consultation evening, though we might assume they can't be bothered, there are, in fact, many reasons that might prevent them from coming into school, such as working a second job or unsocial shift patterns, not having access to or being able to afford a babysitter for their other children or a carer for other members of their family, not being able to afford the cost of transport to school, lacking self-confidence in formal situations, or being fearful of the school premises and the professionals who work there.

The answer: we should put ourselves in parents' shoes. We should be empathetic, not judgemental; we should treat parents with dignity, not disdain. Our job is to support parents who may lack confidence, agency, and solutions. We should, therefore, try emboldening and empowering them.

To give an example, there is little to be gained by talking to a parent about improving their child's attendance until and unless we're willing to offer them practical solutions such as sourcing affordable transport, supplying uniforms and other equipment, or helping establish good morning routines. We need to show parents we are on the same side and that we will stand shoulder-to-shoulder in supporting their child.

Be patient

It takes time to build trust – it's often a war of attrition – and yet mutual trust is vital if we are to engage parents as partners in their child's education. And so, we must think long-term, be strategic, and – above all – be patient. Building trust not only takes time, but it also takes perseverance because it can be tough.

Parents need to believe that we have their best interests – and, more importantly, the best interests of their child – at heart and that we are genuinely there to help, not judge. To achieve that, amongst other strategies, we need a mechanism, ideally several mechanisms, for gathering parents' views and fielding their questions and concerns. An anonymous 'comments box' is one means of doing this. Another is an open forum or headteacher's 'surgery'. Parent surveys are useful ways of gathering feedback and advice. What's crucial is that parents know their views are being listened to.

Consultation does not have to mean compromise. We do not need to act on every suggestion; indeed, sometimes it would be inadvisable to do so. Parents do not always know best, after all. But even inaction needs explaining. I'd suggest a 'You Said, We Did' response which sets out – anonymised – the views shared by parents and our response to those views, whether that's something we've changed or an explanation of why we can't or won't change it.

As well as fielding general questions and comments, we might consider a mechanism for gathering parents' worries – what help do they need with parenting their child? Many parents would not feel comfortable admitting they need help, but some would certainly appreciate the option of posting anonymised problems on which they need advice.

Be open

Even with mechanisms in place for fielding questions and concerns, some parents will still be reluctant to engage with the school directly. Therefore, we need to be open to other means of communication. This might include enlisting volunteers from the local community, trusted figures who can act as parent ambassadors, passing messages between the school and home, and encouraging hard-to-reach parents to take part in school activities.

It also helps if the messages shared with parents are positive. The best messages are centred on the child and their learning. For example, we could start discussions with parents by asking how their child is feeling at school and what they like and dislike. We could ask parents to tell us what their child likes and dislikes outside of school, too, and what they're involved in or doing with their family. We could say we're having difficulty getting their child to read and ask if parents have any suggestions that might help – reminding them that they know their child best. If parents notify us of difficulties at home, we can empathise and then ask if there's anything we can do in school to help rather than making suggestions of what parents can do differently.

Whatever we do to reach out to parents, we need to consider engaging fathers as well as mothers – for this has proven to be particularly effective in improving outcomes for disadvantaged learners. To do this, we should be explicit about the purposes of any events and about the link between such events and improving outcomes.

Be flexible

We need to make it easy for parents to engage. Therefore, we should take account of parents' busy and complicated lives, including their work patterns, when planning events. When scheduling events, we should check when the last bus leaves the bus stop outside school and/or help to arrange carshares for families without their own vehicle. We should offer alternative time slots for those who cannot attend after-school events, such as parents' consultation evenings, and offer alternatives to face-to-face meetings, such as video calls. We should offer to meet parents off-site in a place where parents feel more comfortable, such as in a local café or leisure centre, or indeed in the family home.

As I've already said, schools can be daunting places for some parents. Simply crossing the threshold is too big a barrier to scale. But we can change this by rethinking our reception area. Rather than present our buildings as cold, clinical seats of learning decorated with shields and Ofsted ratings, prospectuses, and rules, we could redesign the foyer as a warm and welcoming café area with comfortable seating, magazines, a water dispenser, and perhaps even a coffee machine. And rather than silence – or classical music – we could play a friendly radio station to soften the mood. And we could make sure all parents can see themselves and their culture reflected in some aspect of the school environment.

Notes

1 Hattie, J. (2008). *Visible learning.* Routledge.
2 Lessof, C., Ross, A., & Brind-Kantar, R. (2019). *Multiple disadvantage and KS4 attainment: Evidence from LSYPE2.* Crown Copyright. https://assets.publishing.service.gov.uk/media/5f33f825d3bf7f1b1ea28df2/LSYPE2_multiple_disadvantage_and_KS4_attainment.pdf
3 Marmot, M. (2020). Health equity in England: The Marmot review 10 years on. *BMJ, 368,* m693. https://doi.org/10.1136/bmj.m693

Community cohesion and coherence

A sense of belonging

Inclusive schools build strong relationships with learners and their families, as well as with their wider community; they foster a sense of belonging and prize the social and emotional development of their learners as much as the academic. When learners have a sense of belonging and are helped to forge healthy, respectful peer relationships, attendance is higher, progress is better, and outcomes are improved. And the positive effects of belonging are amplified for disadvantaged learners and learners with additional and different needs.

Social and emotional skills such as self-awareness (the ability to recognise emotions and thoughts and understand how they influence our behaviour), self-management (the ability to regulate emotions, focus on a task, control impulses and be resilient in the face of failure), social awareness (the ability to show empathy towards others and interact positively with peers and adults), and self-efficacy (the ability to set and achieve goals, and make constructive choices) are important in addressing differences and disadvantages. We know, for example, that disadvantaged children tend to have fewer opportunities to talk about their feelings. Research for the National Children's Bureau[1] shows that children who live in poverty are less likely to talk to someone at home about their worries and are also less likely to talk to their friends about their worries.

According to the Harvard Family Project (2008),[2] "schools cannot do it alone". Schools must work with parents and families and the wider community. This finding is consistent with Bronfenbrenner's[3] concept of the *mesosystem*. However, we also know that families of disadvantaged learners and families of learners with additional and different needs often feel uncomfortable at school. They sometimes have different perspectives from teachers about how to support their children's learning and feel alienated and/or unheard of in school.

Bronfenbrenner's bio-ecological model consists of a series of interacting systems usually depicted as concentric circles:

> The mesosystem consists of the home/family, neighbourhood, school, and so on. The macrosystem includes the culture of the society in which the person lives, national policies, the availability of and access to resources, and so on. The exosystem consists of contexts that extend beyond the immediate environment of the child such as home and

DOI: 10.4324/9781003520634-17

school but which, nevertheless, affect development. Parents' workplaces are part of the exosystem and if these involve long or irregular working hours, are stressful and do not provide adequate compensation, parents are less likely to have the time and psychological and financial resources to support children than in workplaces where the opposite is the case. Bronfenbrenner later added the chronosystem to the model, acknowledging the importance of time, developmentally and historically (Bronfenbrenner & Morris, 2006). He argued that there were interconnections between the various contexts or settings in which the person developed.

The key takeaway is that Bronfenbrenner argues that schools should look to engage with a learner's wider family and community, not just parents. He suggested that grandparents and siblings also play a part in a child's education and that by reaching out to the whole family and wider community, not just parents, schools can foster mutual trust.

The French sociologist Pierre Bourdieu coined the now-familiar term *cultural capital,* which is the knowledge that confers status and recognition. This knowledge and experience reflect the values of those who wield power in society.

Bourdieu also coined the term *social capital,* which refers to the connections people have or the networks to which they belong. These connections allow them to gain access to and participate in various domains. For example, middle-class families utilise their networks to share information and knowledge about schooling and to advocate for themselves and their children.

Cultural and social capital are connected to the amount of economic capital – wealth – people possess.

But it's Bourdieu's concepts of capital, field, habitus, and doxa that are perhaps more instructive here.

Field refers to social spaces where the different forms of capital circulate and are reproduced. For example, a school may be considered a field.

Habitus is a system of internalised structures, schemes of perception, conception, and action common to all members of the same group or class.

Doxa are the assumptions or self-evident truths within cultural or social groups. For example, in some contexts, teachers assume that disadvantaged families are not interested in their children's learning and do not actively support them.

The best community engagement initiatives seek to improve family–school partnerships and reflect Bronfenbrenner's conception of the importance of connections between the different zones involved in a child's development and learning, home and school. Familiarising families with school life is important, but a better strategy is to help families promote learning at home.

The best community engagement initiatives attempt to address system blockage between families and schools, mainly by sharing knowledge with families as a means to enhance children's learning and development in schools. This system blockage might take the form of educating families about valuing education or about educating teachers about family circumstances and bringing the community into schools. This involves close collaboration between families and schools from conceptualisation to implementation.

Although homes and schools are different fields with different codes and practices, the most effective strategies increase the overlap between them; they create a shared habitus and a common set of doxa. Schools need to make it more explicit to families that the knowledge children need to acquire to be successful both at school and in later life. The cultural capital and habitus that children from culturally, linguistically, and socio-economically diverse homes bring with them are valuable, and schools need to do more to recognise and include them.

Talking to learners' lived experiences

In one of my opening keynotes at an inclusion conference in London, I began by exploring the effects of Photonism on learners with Legatis.

I explained to the gathered audience that Photonism had an adverse impact on all learners with SEND, but those with Legatis were disproportionately affected. I referenced some data to prove my point but was met with a sea of blank faces, so I sought a useful comparison: I said that the line on the graph I was referring to was similar in shape to the outline of the famous New Fountainville building in Smithson Square, Newmanham. The chimney to the back-left of the building, as you look at it from the square, represents learners with Legatis – a clear outlier in the data, thus underlining the detrimental impact of Photonism on learners with Legatis.

As my audience frantically searched Google, fearing they'd missed an important aspect of SEND affecting some learners in their schools, or else suspected they – or more likely I – were having 'a moment', I came clean: I'd made it all up. There is no such thing as Photonism or Legatis.

So, why did I talk such gibberish, you may ask? I wanted my audience, a couple of hundred experienced SENDCos and school leaders, to know first-hand what it felt like to be excluded from the curriculum. They had no prior knowledge of Photonism nor Legatis for the simple reason it was all nonsense, so they did not feel included in my 'classroom'. The content of my 'lesson' meant nothing to them; it didn't talk about their prior knowledge or life experiences. Some of them told me over coffee afterwards that they'd begun to panic because they'd thought they'd missed something important; others said they'd begun to shrink into their seats, scared of being the only person in the room not to possess some vital prior knowledge.

Of course, we often impart information to learners in class with which they are unfamiliar. That's why they're at school, after all: to encounter new information and learn new skills. But to help them access and process what's new, we often make use of analogies and metaphors to compare the unfamiliar to the familiar. In other words, we help learners connect their prior knowledge to new knowledge, to forge new schema or mental maps. That's why I compared the data with which my audience was unfamiliar (because I had invented it) to something familiar and concrete – the New Fountainville building in Smithson Square. But my analogy didn't work either because I'd made that building up, too. There is no New Fountainville building, nor is there a Smithson Square, or at least not in Newmanham, because that place doesn't exist either. And so, my analogy didn't 'land'. My audience could not use their prior knowledge of the outline of a familiar building to imagine the plotline of a graph because that prior knowledge was not present in their long-term memory. In this case, it was by design; often, in our classrooms, this happens by accident because we are unaware of the gaps in learners' prior knowledge and life experiences.

Knowledge begets knowledge. The more you know, the easier it is to know more. But the opposite is also true: the less you know, the harder it is to know more. And thus, the learners who start school at a disadvantage in terms of their prior knowledge (what some would call 'cultural capital'), are further disadvantaged by the school system and fall further and further behind.

In order to include the excluded and to ensure we bring the community into our curriculum, I posit a three-point plan:

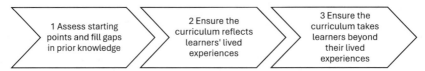

Figure 13.1 Three steps for bringing the community into the curriculum

Step 1: Assess starting points and fill gaps in prior knowledge

The first step towards including the excluded and bringing the community into the curriculum is to be more mindful of our learners' prior knowledge and starting points – or rather, the gaps in their prior knowledge – and then work hard to fill those gaps. This might require the pre-teaching of key concepts or words; it might necessitate the use of adaptive teaching strategies such as task-scaffolding to make our curriculum accessible to all, and it might entail the provision of additional interventions such as mentoring or funded access to extra-curricular activities to help equip learners with the cultural capital they lack.

Step 2: Ensure the curriculum reflects learners' lived experiences

The second step towards including the excluded is to ensure that the content of our curriculum reflects our learners' own lives and experiences. We want them to see themselves and their community mirrored in our curriculum so that they can access it, process it, understand it, and know that it talks to them. This might take the form of ensuring greater levels of representation – both in the content we teach (the topics we choose to cover and the texts and resources we use to help deliver that content) and the examples we deploy in our daily teaching (such as analogies, metaphors, and stories); but it might also require us to think about how representative our school staff are of our learners. Do learners see themselves not only in *what* is taught but also in *who* teaches them? Do we co-construct our curriculum with families?

Step 3: Ensure the curriculum takes learners beyond their lived experiences

The third step towards including the excluded is to ensure our curriculum celebrates diversity because mirroring our learners' lived experiences isn't enough. Once we have made sure our curriculum and the examples we use to illustrate that curriculum are more representative of our learners, we then need to take our learners beyond their lived experiences to visit new worlds, meet new people, and celebrate differences and diversity. This might mean rethinking our curriculum to ensure it challenges learners' preconceptions and prejudices and that it promotes empathy and tolerance; it might mean decolonising our curriculum and including more voices from across the social strata and from as many different cultures as possible.

What does this look like in practice?

The National Literacy Trust's 2022 research on diversity[4] found that two in five (38.9%) children and young people think it's difficult to find books with characters or people like them, increasing to one in two (53.1%) children aged 8 to 11. While just over one in three (34.9%) children and young people from White backgrounds say they struggle to see themselves in what they read, this increases to nearly one in two (45.2%) children and young people from Black ethnic backgrounds. More than two in five (42.5%) of those receiving free school meals report finding it difficult to see themselves in books compared with just over one in three (35.2%) of their peers who do not receive free school meals.

And the same is also true of our school curriculum. The already disadvantaged or disenfranchised are further excluded by a curriculum that does not talk to them.

One strategy we can use to ensure our curriculum talks to our learners' lived experiences is *schema theory*.

A *schema* is a mental structure or framework that helps learners organise and interpret information. Schemas influence how people perceive, think about, and remember information. Schemas can be activated automatically and unconsciously, which means they can influence our perceptions and behaviours without us realising it. For example, if someone has a schema for a 'restaurant', they might automatically think of certain things such as tables, chairs, menus, waiters, and food. This schema helps them quickly recognise and understand new restaurants they encounter. Schemas can also be influenced by cultural and social factors, as well as individual differences. For instance, someone from one culture might have a different schema for a 'family' than someone from another culture.

Keene and Zimmerman (1997)[5] argued that learners understand curriculum content better when they make three kinds of connections:

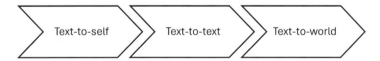

Figure 13.2 Schema theory – three connections

Text-to-self connections are made when learners make highly personal associations between what's being taught in class and their own lived experiences.

Text-to-text connections are made when learners are reminded of other parts of the curriculum and their prior knowledge of the same or similar subject.

Text-to-world connections are made when learners make larger associations between what's being taught in class and the world beyond their own lived experiences from knowledge that might have been garnered from television and films, newspapers and magazines, and the internet and social media.

Connections can occur naturally, but it's best not left to chance. Rather, we should encourage learners to make connections by modelling the process for them and by prompting them. The following prompts may be of use:

Text-to-self:

● What aspect of my own life does this remind me of?

● In what way is this different from my own life and experiences?

● Has something like this ever happened to me?

● How did I feel when I encountered this information?

Text-to-text:

● What other knowledge have I been taught that reminds me of this?

● In what way is this similar to other things I've learned?

● In what way is this different from what I've learned previously?

Text-to-world:

● What aspects of the real world does this remind me of?

● In what way is this different from events in the real world?

● What have I read/seen/been told about the real world that's relevant here?

● What contextual information might help me understand this curriculum content better?

However, Harvey and Goudvis (2000)[6] warn that merely making connections is not enough because learners may make tangential connections that confuse and distract them from the information at hand. Accordingly, learners need to be challenged to analyse how their connections are contributing to their understanding of the curriculum.

Once we've made sure our curriculum reflects our learners' lived experiences, we then need to make sure it takes them beyond those experiences.

As I've already said, the best schools reflect their local communities; they bring their communities into their schools and take learners out into those communities. The best schools also look beyond their local communities and regard themselves as part of the national and international conversation. These schools teach learners how to be active members of their communities and how to be good citizens of the world.

We can help learners move beyond their lived experiences by ensuring the texts we teach include role models from all walks of life and that the examples and case studies we use include minority voices. We can bring a diverse range of people into our school to give guest talks and to co-teach parts of the curriculum, and we can take learners out of school to visit the corners of our community – or the wider world – that would otherwise be out-of-bounds to them.

Curriculums that are reflective of learners' own lives lend credence to those lives and make them feel included and – for want of a better word – 'normal' or accepted. But, curriculums that are also reflective of other lives different from learners' own help them to understand how other people live and lend empathy and compassion.

In other words, a good curriculum acts as a **mirror** – reflecting learners' lives back at them so they feel included, *and* as a **window** – allowing learners to see other lives different from their own so they appreciate diversity.

Extra-curricular activities

Another way of engaging the community in the curriculum – and of engaging learners in their local community – is through the extra-curricular programme.

It is important, though, that we provide all learners with equal access to extra-curricular activities. We can achieve this, in part, through more targeted funding for those who would otherwise be denied these opportunities. And we can achieve this by auditing who accesses extra-curricular activities and ascertaining what barriers prevent some learners from taking part and then removing those barriers. For example, the timings may be a problem or access to transport may be the issue. Or it may be the cost of additional equipment or educational visits that puts some learners off taking part.

When done well and made accessible to those most in need, extra-curricular activities can connect schools to their communities and expand learners' life experiences.

A paper by the Social Mobility Commission called *An Unequal Playing Field: Extra-Curricular Activities, Soft Skills and Social Mobility* argued that "The breadth of extra-curricular activities, spanning the musical, artistic, social and sporting domains, are widely considered valuable life experiences that should be open to all young people, regardless of background or where they happen to live".[7]

In *The Working Classroom*, I argued that extra-curricular activities have three purposes:

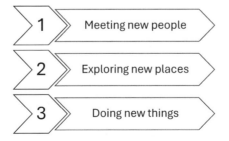

Figure 13.3 The three purposes of extra-curricular activities

Apart from the inherent value of extra-curricular activities, the Social Mobility Commission report asserted that "young people can also develop positive tangible outcomes from these

experiences of interacting and working with others . . . which could benefit them in later life".
However, the report's authors also said that access to extra-curricular activities for disadvantaged learners and those with additional needs was not yet universal, and the impact of such activities on this cohort was not yet good enough.

To help improve the situation, the report set out four key findings and four recommendations for policy and practice:

1. **Extra-curricular activities are important to young people and result in a range of positive outcomes.** Research findings suggest that "extra-curricular activities are important in developing soft (especially social) skills as well as being associated with a range of other positive outcomes".[8] Regardless of instrumental outcomes,

   > extra-curricular activities [are] hugely valuable to young people themselves in ways that are not quantifiable [because they] boost young people's confidence to interact socially with others; extend their social networks; and provide them with new skills and abilities. Above all, they offer an important space to have fun and relax.

2. **Opportunities to take part in extra-curricular activities are unequally distributed.**

   > Wide parts of life experience gained from extra-curricular activities are unavailable for the most marginalised groups in society. Opportunities to participate are driven by household income, school attended, gender, ethnicity and geographic location. Household income is by far the most important factor driving gaps in participation, with children from the poorest households much less likely to take part in all types of extra-curricular activities, but especially music classes and sport.

   > The report also found that "independent schools [are] likely to offer an unparalleled breadth and range of activities compared to state schools", thus further impacting social mobility.

3. **Employers in the UK labour market increasingly demand soft skills, which could be an important factor in driving intergenerational social mobility.** The report notes that "demand exists for soft skills from employers in the UK labour market [and that there is] evidence of an association between soft skills . . . and intergenerational social mobility". Indeed, the researchers "found a correlation between higher levels of some soft skills (readiness to learn, problem-solving, and planning skills) and upward social mobility defined as an individual having higher educational attainment than their parents".

4. **New programmes and initiatives are required to widen opportunities to participate in extra-curricular activities.** The report proffered four recommendations aimed at levelling the playing field and improving access to a breadth of life experience provided by extra-curricular activities. These "cover both national-level policy as well as the delivery of activities in practice". The recommendations are:

   1. Introduce a national extra-curricular bursary scheme.

   2. Provide funding to develop and extend third-sector initiatives that successfully facilitate access to extra-curricular activities.

3. Increase the organisational capacity of schools to support their extra-curricular provision and improve information on the availability of activities in local areas.

4. Improve data collection and carry out further research into the nature of soft skills developed and deployed across different settings.

Whether we use extra-curricular activities to forge closer connections with the community, to build learners' cultural capital, or to ensure that learners are afforded opportunities to gain new skills for learning's sake, or indeed for all of these purposes, it is important that we evaluate the impact of our extra-curricular provision to ensure it is providing quality and value for money. Participation rates can be a helpful indicator of this, but case studies of learners who take part are also a useful way to showcase their commitment to those activities, as well as demonstrate the development of skills such as resilience and, ultimately, the academic impact of extra-curricular provision.

Notes

1 Gibb, J., Rix, K., Wallace, E., Fitzsimmons, E., & Mostafa, T. (2016). *Poverty and children's personal and social relationships. Secondary analysis of Millennium Cohort Study data, supported by the Joseph Rowntree Foundation.* National Children's Bureau. https://www.ncb.org.uk/sites/default/files/uploads/files/poverty_and_children_s_personal_and_social_relationships_-_final_report_-_march_2016.pdf

2 https://archive.globalfrp.org/evaluation/the-evaluation-exchange/issue-archive/building-the-future-of-family-involvement

3 Bronfenbrenner, U. (1979). *The ecology of human development: Experiments by nature and design.* Harvard University Press.

4 https://literacytrust.org.uk/research-services/research-reports/seeing-yourself-in-what-you-read-diversity-and-children-and-young-peoples-reading-in-2022/

5 Keane, E., & Zimmerman, S. (1997). *Mosaic of thought: Teaching comprehension in a reader's workshop.* Heinemann.

6 Harvey, S., & Goudvis, A. (2000). *Strategies that work: Teaching comprehension to enhance understanding.* Stenhouse Publishers.

7 Donnelly, M., Lažetić, P., Sandoval-Hernandez, A., Kumar, K., & Whewall, S. (2022). *An unequal playing field: Extra-curricular activities, soft skills and social mobility* (p. 2). Social Mobility Commission. https://assets.publishing.service.gov.uk/government/uploads/system/uploads/attachment_data/file/818679/An_Unequal_Playing_Field_report.pdf

8 Donnelly, M. et al. (2022). *An unequal playing field: Extra-curricular activities, soft skills and social mobility* (p. 2).

14 Community and the curriculum

The 4Ps

Another aspect of community is making sure the school curriculum talks to its community and is truly inclusive of its community. This, in turn, requires building a community of teachers to work together to improve the quality of education they provide and to ensure that high standards are delivered consistently in every corner of the school. No learner should be allowed to fall through the net; every learner should receive their entitlement to high-quality teaching every day.

This is something I've been working on with one of the schools I support. We've sought to ensure that every learner is enthusiastic about attending school and motivated to learn, is challenged and engaged by an ambitious curriculum, and is supported to make good progress and be prepared for their next steps, irrespective of their starting points, backgrounds, and additional and different needs.

To help them on their journey, I formulated a framework called the 4Ps. The idea was this: I wanted a simple way of capturing all the key actions on their school improvement plan, a means for teachers to self-evaluate their current practice to identify their professional development needs, and a shared language with which to articulate their vision and values.

I settled on the 4Ps after a review of their current practice and after lots of in-depth conversations with staff and learners. The 4Ps are:

Figure 14.1 The 4Ps

Here's a brief overview of each P before I delve into the detail . . .

1. Purpose

Purpose is about planning an ambitious curriculum to which all learners have access – including, with appropriate support, disadvantaged learners and those with SEND. It's about making sure the curriculum addresses social disadvantages and gives learners access to the highest levels of knowledge, skills, and experience.

The process by which we hope school leaders and teachers will achieve this is as follows: first, they will identify the knowledge and skills that learners need to thrive in the future; second, they will plan and sequence the curriculum to ensure progression, using 'threshold concepts' (or similar) to assess progress over time; third, they will ensure there is clarity about the knowledge and skills to be learned – in other words, each teacher will be clear about what they expect learners to learn and *why* that is important; fourth, there will be a logic to the order and organisation of lessons – what is taught today will build upon and extend what was taught yesterday and will be built upon and extended by what is taught tomorrow; sixth, prior knowledge will be activated through planned (daily) retrieval practice and then will be added to, forging ever more complex mental maps in long-term memory.

The first P – purpose – is also about teachers articulating the bigger picture to explain to learners what they are learning, why they are learning it, and what they will do with that learning later. This, we hope, will help build learners' intrinsic motivation. It will also ensure that learners have the requisite knowledge to be able to understand new concepts and process new abstract information within the context of what is already familiar and concrete.

The content taught will be ambitious, broad, and balanced. There will be high expectations of what all learners can learn, and the knowledge, skills, and behaviours learners acquire will allow them to progress to the next stage of their learning journey. The content covered in class will be sufficiently broad so that it prepares learners for what comes next, but it will also be taught with appropriate depth to ensure genuine understanding and aid transferability.

There are five criteria associated with purpose:

1. I teach an appropriate and ambitious curriculum to all my learners and ensure it fills knowledge gaps.

2. I teach the knowledge, skills, and behaviours that my learners need to progress to the next stage of their education, employment, and lives.

3. What I teach represents excellence in my subject field and will prepare learners for future success.

4. I sequence learning to ensure my learners make progress, and I use retrieval practice to activate and build upon prior learning.

5. I tell my learners what they are expected to learn, why that matters, and how they will use it later.

2. Pitch

Pitch is about making sure learners know more and remember what they have learned. It is also about how learners are helped to become increasingly independent and resilient as learners. It's about making sure all learners are taught the same curriculum, thus ensuring equality, but that those with additional needs are supported through adaptive teaching strategies, such

146 Why School Doesn't Work for Every Child

as task scaffolding, thus ensuring equity. In short, pitch is about making sure that learners who start with *less* are given *more* help to access the curriculum and to achieve in line with their peers.

To achieve this, learners' starting points will be ascertained and gaps in prior knowledge – and any misunderstandings or mistakes learners bring with them – will be identified and filled. Next, all learners will be helped to access the same task, and any additional scaffolding will fall away over time, ensuring learners become increasingly independent. There will be opportunities for retrieval practice and thus the building of mental maps or schema in every lesson. Whilst the shape and form of this retrieval practice – and when it happens within the lesson – will be dependent on the context and left to each teacher's professional judgement, it will frequently happen to prevent knowledge decay and to help learners connect prior learning to new learning.

In lessons, all learners, not just the higher-performing learners, will be stretched and challenged – both in terms of the content being taught and in the feedback given to help learners improve further.

Learners will also be supported in developing research and study skills relevant to their learning and developing wider knowledge and skills beyond the school curriculum.

Expectations of all learners will be high, both academically and in terms of their attitudes to learning.

There are five criteria associated with pitch:

1. I continually improve and update both my subject knowledge and pedagogical knowledge so that I know what excellence looks like in practice, and I use my knowledge to ensure I *teach to the top* for all learners.

2. I teach all my learners an appropriate and ambitious curriculum (thus ensuring equality), but I also make sure that those with additional needs are supported through adaptive teaching strategies, such as task scaffolding (thus ensuring equity).

3. I assess my learners' starting points and identify any gaps in their prior knowledge – as well as any misunderstandings they bring with them – and use this information to stretch and challenge all my learners through the level of task difficulty and in the feedback that I give them.

4. I plan frequent opportunities for retrieval practice and, thus, the building of schema.

5. I support all my learners to develop the research and study skills they need in lessons and to develop wider knowledge and skills beyond the curriculum.

3. Pace

Pace is about there being a sense of urgency in lessons – so that no learner is allowed to sit back and relax or be passive, but rather, all learners are engaged, active participants in the process of learning.

To ensure appropriate pace and learner participation, teachers – aided by a whole-school culture that comes from the top in the form of visible, supportive leaders – will create and maintain a disciplined environment with clear expectations for behaviour, and learners will be helped to stay motivated and to embody positive attitudes to learning. There will be a strong focus on attendance and punctuality, and bullying, harassment, and discrimination will not be accepted – any issues will be quickly and consistently dealt with.

Teachers will use their subject knowledge to enthuse learners with clear and insightful explanations, during which they will pre-empt misconceptions and questions. Then, they will model excellence and, whilst doing so, think aloud – making their invisible thought processes and decision-making (and the making of mistakes) visible to learners, thus making their implicit expertise explicit to the novice learner and modelling metacognition and self-regulation.

Teachers will engage learners in co-construction, producing a model together. Learners will provide substantive content whilst the teacher asks probing questions, drip-feeds technical vocabulary, and passes the baton between learners so they can comment on and add to each other's contributions.

Teachers will use questioning effectively to engage learners and to provide ongoing formative feedback.

Lesson activities will be varied over time – with teacher explanations and modelling 'chunked' with questioning, practice activities, or group discussions which will aid learners' retention and increase their attention spans.

Ongoing formative assessment and feedback will be used to support the teaching of the curriculum and provide information to learners on which they can and do act.

There are five criteria associated with pace:

1. My classroom is a disciplined environment in which there are clear expectations for behaviour, guided by the whole-school culture, and in which learners are motivated and develop positive attitudes to learning.

2. I enthuse my learners with clear and insightful explanations, then model excellence and, whilst doing so, think aloud.

3. I ensure lesson activities are planned to gradually hand ownership to my learners so that they can contribute equitably and, through this, become increasingly independent.

4. I use questioning effectively to engage learners and challenge and deepen their thinking, as well as to check understanding and provide ongoing formative feedback.

5. I give learners feedback only when I allow time for them to process it and act upon it. I then celebrate the progress they make. I use the outcomes of assessments to inform the pace and pitch of my teaching, and I am unafraid to stray from the plan and be flexible in my delivery.

4. Progress

And finally, the fourth P is progress. The commitment here is that all assessments will be sense-checked for purpose, process, and validity to ensure teachers only assess learners when it will have a demonstrable impact on their progress. There's also a commitment to ensure all teacher marking is meaningful, manageable, and motivating, thus protecting teacher workload and wellbeing.

Progress will be expedited when learners know how, when, and why they will be assessed and how prior learning will be activated and built upon. Learners will only be assessed when an assessment will lead to feedback, and feedback will only be given when there is time carved out in the lesson for them to process it, question it, and act upon it.

The results of assessments will be used as learning opportunities – often in the form of whole class feedback on the most common errors – rather than simply to draw lines in the sand.

Learners will be given planned opportunities to extend their experiences, including keeping themselves healthy and safe and developing plans for their next steps.

When good practice is embedded, all learners will make good in-year progress from their individual starting points, and those identified as being at risk of not making enough progress will be supported in a timely manner, and targeted, evidence-informed interventions will prove impactful.

Ultimately, as a measure of overall success, all learners in school will be prepared for the next stage of their education and lives, and they will progress to high-quality destinations.

There are five criteria associated with progress:

1. My learners know how, when, and why they will be assessed and how prior learning will be activated and built upon.

2. The results of assessments are used as learning opportunities – often in the form of whole-class feedback on the most common errors.

3. My learners are given planned opportunities to extend their experiences, including keeping themselves healthy and safe and developing their plans for their next steps.

4. My learners receive effective advice and guidance to help ensure they follow a relevant pathway and are prepared for the future.

5. My learners make good in-year progress from their individual starting points, and those identified as being at risk of not making enough progress are supported in a timely manner, and interventions are impactful.

In the remainder of this chapter and in the chapter that follows, I'll delve deeper into each of the 4Ps.

1 Purpose

The holy trinity of planning: Ambitious, progressive, preparatory

Inclusive curriculum plans are threefold:

1. They are *ambitious* for all learners in that they embody high expectations and excellence.

Figure 14.2 Features of an inclusive curriculum plan

2. They are *progressive* in that there is continuity so that what's taught today builds upon and extends what was taught yesterday and builds towards what will be taught tomorrow.

3. They are *preparatory* in that they equip learners with the knowledge, skills, and behaviours they need to succeed at the next stage of their lives.

Making the curriculum ambitious starts with equality . . .

If we dumb down or reduce the curriculum for some learners because of their starting points, backgrounds, or additional and different needs, then we would be guilty of deepening those existing differences and disadvantages rather than using the curriculum as a tool for social justice. Therefore, we should teach the same curriculum to all learners. We should afford all learners the opportunity to be exposed to excellence in every subject discipline and to be given an equal chance of succeeding in the same tasks.

As well as representing excellence, the best curriculums represent our learners. In other words, they talk to our learners' lived experiences so that they can see themselves and their lives reflected in the content we teach as well as in the examples and analogies we use to teach it. This is important if learners are to engage in school life and if they are to believe that they have a part to play in education. Representation is about inclusion.

Once we have made sure our curriculum is inclusive, we need it to celebrate diversity. In other words, we want it to take learners beyond their lived experiences and teach them about people who are different from them, including those from other cultures and backgrounds. Celebrating diversity helps foster empathy and understanding; it helps prepare learners for future success.

The purpose of education is to enable all learners to acquire knowledge that takes them beyond their experience, knowledge which many will not have access to at home or in the communities in which they live.

Equality gives way to equity . . .

So, it starts with equality – teaching the same ambitious, inclusive, and diverse curriculum to all – but equality is still not enough. Equality needs to give way to equity . . .

If we gave every learner *exactly* the same uniform to wear, it might fit a small proportion of our learner population, but it'll be too big or too small for the vast majority of learners. So, whilst we want all learners to wear the same uniform in order to promote equality, we must ensure that learners are given uniforms in a size that fits them.

Equity is about teaching all learners the same curriculum – and requiring them to complete the same tasks in lessons – but then making sure the curriculum fits them by tailoring it (pun intended) to meet their individual needs.

Most often, this adaptation takes the form of task scaffolding. Scaffolds are short-term tweaks we make to tasks to help all learners access them. Scaffolds might take the form of more detailed or chunked instructions, partially completed tasks or worked examples, the reteaching of key concepts, a bank of keywords and definitions, support from an additional adult, and so on. The key to making scaffolds successful is that they are reduced over time to avoid perpetuating learned helplessness.

Making the curriculum progressive starts with sequencing . . .

Next, to ensure our curriculum is *progressive*, we need to sequence learning over time. Sequencing is about activating and building on prior knowledge and building towards our ambitious end points. The best curriculums bake in increasing challenges and enable learners to build ever-more complex mental maps of information. The best curriculums have a logic to their order and organisation – like sculpting a statue by gradually chiselling away at a block of stone to reveal ever-more complex detail – but are not linear; rather, they are cyclical because they return to prior learning to ensure it does not decay and to connect it to new learning.

Sequencing works well when we know what was taught previously. In other words, we need to find out what learners should already know and be able to do and what likely misconceptions they'll bring with them to the classroom. Then, we identify the checkpoints through which learners must pass on their journey through our curriculum – what does good progress look like at each juncture? What should learners know and do at each stage? Once we have this shape set out – perhaps in the form of a progression map – we need to decide how progress will be assessed and what we will do with the data to ensure all learners are supported and that we maintain the integrity of our curriculum sequencing – in other words, we need to know how to support those who have fallen behind without allowing the gap between them and their higher-performing peers to widen.

Peer teaching is a great way to do this. Rather than allow higher-performing learners to rush too far ahead whilst others flounder, peer teaching ensures that all learners remain at the same stage of our sequence but that all learners are meaningfully engaged. Those who are peer-taught are helped to understand key concepts by having them retaught by someone else, perhaps using more accessible language or analogies. Those who are peer-teaching deepen their understanding of key concepts by engaging in retrieval practice and by having to explain those concepts to someone else.

Making the curriculum preparatory starts with purpose . . .

Next, to ensure our curriculum is *preparatory*, we need to know where learners are going and what they will need to know and do when they get there. We also need to consider outcomes in the widest sense of the word – what will a successful learner look like at the end? What will they know and be able to do, what qualities and traits will they possess, how will they behave, and what values will they hold dear?

Preparing learners for future success is about looking beyond a subject specification rather than teaching to the test. It is about identifying the more ambitious end points of a great education and personal development. What, other than a good qualification (which remains important) will our learners need in their toolkit in order to be well-equipped for the next stage of their education and lives?

Preparing learners for the future is also about identifying the skills they need and then explicitly planning and teaching those skills. Skill development is, I think, two-fold: firstly, there are the skills that learners need now in order to access and achieve in school – these comprise study skills such as note-taking and research, as well as independent learning skills such as metacognition; secondly, there are the skills that learners will need outside of school in order to play a full part in the world – these comprise character traits such as resilience, determination, compassion, communication including oracy, confidence and self-esteem, empathy, the ability to keep safe and healthy, forward-planning, organisation and time management, teamwork and so on.

Often, we leave the development of skills to chance rather than identify the skills that learners need both now and in the future, then explicitly plan and teach them.

Sharing is caring . . .

Finally, once we've achieved all the previous, we need to share it with learners. In other words, we need to articulate the bigger picture to explain to learners:

1. What they are learning.

2. Why they are learning it.

3. What they will do with that learning later.

Sharing the bigger picture will help build learners' intrinsic motivation. It will also ensure that learners have the requisite knowledge to be able to understand new concepts and process new abstract information within the context of what is already familiar and concrete.

The big picture is a learner-friendly version of our curriculum plan and sequence; it shows learners how learning connects and builds over time, how their progress will be assessed, and what real-world applications their learning will have in the future.

Purpose and motivation are also borne of future-planning. We want learners to have an idea of where they are headed and how they will get there. This involves careers education and the development of employability skills. It involves work experience, including work placements. And it involves making explicit connections between what we teach and the world of work.

Purpose breeds motivation. As such, the more we can articulate a clear goal to learners – explaining what they're learning, why they're learning it, and how they'll use that learning later – the more we can plan an ambitious, progressive, and preparatory curriculum with excellence at its heart, the more purpose and motivation we will foster in our learners and the more successful they will be.

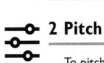 2 Pitch

To pitch learning in learners' struggle zones – what will cause thinking, be hard but achievable – we need to know what excellence looks like. And this requires both subject knowledge and pedagogical content knowledge, knowing our *stuff* (to use a technical term) and knowing how to teach that stuff in a way that makes sense to learners.

This 'dual professionalism' requires a planned programme of continuing professional development (CPD) which enables us to keep our subject knowledge and pedagogical content knowledge up to date. The best CPD balances external expertise with internal peer-to-peer support. The best CPD balances innovation (a focus on new ideas) with mastery (providing opportunities for teachers to deepen their knowledge and understanding of existing ideas and to practice existing strategies). And the best CPD is sustained over the long term and is evaluated to ensure it is having a demonstrable impact in the classroom.

As well as CPD, knowing what excellence looks like also requires networking – both internally in the form of subject teams peer-assessing learners' work to moderate judgements – and externally in the form of working with other schools and, indeed, subject associations to benchmark standards beyond the school gates.

Knowledge is power . . .

Once we know what excellence looks like, we need to teach to the top for all learners. Why? Because knowledge of long-term memory is essential in helping learners make sense of new information. Amongst other things, it improves reading comprehension and critical thinking.

Knowledge in long-term memory is essential for reading comprehension because, although the ability to decode words is transferable to different texts, learners are more likely to understand a text if they have prior knowledge about the topic. Put simply, the more you know about a topic, the more effectively you can read a text on that topic and understand it. If I asked you to read a text on, say, nuclear physics or macroeconomics, you'd probably struggle to make full sense of it because some of the words would be unfamiliar, and many of the concepts certainly would be. However, if I asked you to read an article on teaching strategies, you'd probably fare well, bringing your prior knowledge to bear on the words and meanings contained within the text.

Knowledge in long-term memory is also essential for critical thinking. Critical thinking cannot occur if a learner does not have sufficient foundational knowledge of the topic being discussed. In history, for example, for learners to be able to reason effectively about chronology and cause and effect, they must know enough curriculum content. Teaching learners about history in an abstract way doesn't work as well as arming them with lots of knowledge with which to better understand the way the world works. In maths, learners need to be taught through worked examples rather than unstructured problems. And in science, learners need to be taught the knowledge gained through scientific discovery, not necessarily *how* science discovered that knowledge. Facts matter. Put simply, you cannot be critical about something of which you are ignorant.

Not only is factual knowledge essential to reading comprehension and critical thinking, but it's also a means of closing the gap between the attainment of disadvantaged learners and their non-disadvantaged peers, and this is the reason we should teach to the top for all, not just higher-performing learners.

Start at the beginning . . .

Educational disadvantage starts early – certainly before a child enters formal education. One of the reasons for this is that children born into families who read books, newspapers, and magazines, visit museums, art galleries, zoos, and stately homes and gardens, take regular holidays, watch the nightly news and documentaries, and talk – around the dinner table, on weekend walks, in the car – about current affairs and about what they're reading or doing or watching – develop 'cultural capital'. In other words, they acquire an awareness of the world around them, an understanding of how life works, and – crucially – a language with which to explain it . . . all of which provides a solid foundation on which these children can build further knowledge, skills, and understanding.

Those children not born and raised in such knowledge-rich environments don't do as well in school because new knowledge and skills have nothing to 'stick' to or build upon. Put simply, the more you know, the easier it is to know more, so the culturally rich will always stay ahead of the impoverished, and the gap between rich and poor will continue to grow as children travel through our education system.

Once we accept the need to teach to the top for all, we need to know where 'the top' is.

Teaching to the top . . .

Teaching to the top is about pitching learning at what the highest-performing learners in a class will be able to do with time, effort, and support.

One of the main problems with teaching to the top is that some learners fear hard work. Therefore, we need to eliminate – or at least mitigate – learners' feelings of fear and hesitation by creating a classroom environment which encourages the making of mistakes as a sign of learning and which explicitly says (through our choice of language, modelling, thinking aloud, and the routines we engage in) there is nothing to fear by trying your best and pushing yourself to do hard work.

To promote challenge in the classroom, we need to reduce the threat level – we need to ensure no one feels humiliated if they fall short of a challenge. Rather, they need to know they will learn from the experience and perform better next time.

What else can we do to ensure the pitch is appropriate?

Firstly, we can put blocks in the way of learners' initial learning (or encoding) to bolster their subsequent storage and retrieval strength.

Secondly, we can 'chunk' information, ensuring we teach knowledge before skill. And we can link new learning with prior learning so that learners can cheat their limited working memories.

Thirdly, we can provide opportunities for our learners to engage in deliberate practice, repeating learning at least three times but doing so in a different way each time, allowing learners to do something new with the learning every time they encounter it to forge myriad connections and improve 'transfer'.

Of course, to set the right level of pitch, we also need to identify learners' struggle zones (perhaps using low-stakes quizzes, hinge questions, exit tickets, etc.).

One way to pitch learning appropriately is to activate prior knowledge, which enables us to uncover and unpack any gaps in learners' knowledge as well as any misconceptions they may have. We can then ensure all the class are 'on the same page' and are following the same steps.

What's more, activating prior knowledge helps join up the curriculum in learners' minds because they can see how they use and expand the knowledge and skills they learnt previously as they progress through school, and this provides intrinsic motivation because they can see the purpose of what they learn and can begin to understand the usefulness of curriculum content. Thus, it helps achieve the first of our 4Ps: purpose.

Assessing prior knowledge . . .

There are several ways in which we can assess learners' prior knowledge as they travel through our curriculum. For example, we could begin each new topic with a KWL chart, which is a diagnostic technique and a means of acquiring data on learners' starting points by asking learners at the beginning of a lesson or new topic to identify what they already know (or think they know) about what they are about to study, what they want to learn about the topic, and, as the unit unfolds, the knowledge and skills that they begin to acquire.

An alternative to this is to begin a topic with an initial assessment, perhaps a low-stakes multiple-choice quiz. The results of these pre-tests can yield invaluable evidence about learners' prior knowledge and misconceptions and, when repeated at various stages of the teaching sequence, can provide evidence of learners' growing knowledge and understanding.

Regardless of the approach taken, information from diagnostic assessments can help us ensure that lessons are more responsive to learners' needs and their existing knowledge base, and so that knowledge builds upon knowledge.

Pitch is about having high expectations of all learners; it's about establishing a set of clear rules and routines. As well as having high expectations of our learners we should insist that our learners have high expectations of themselves because only by believing in yourself and in your own ability to get better will you do so. So, what does this look like in practice?

Developing the right mindset . . .

Firstly, learners should have a growth mindset and believe that they can get better at anything if they work hard. This means having a thirst for knowledge, this means accepting that work needs to be drafted and redrafted, and this means following the maxim that if it isn't excellent, it isn't finished (never settling for work that is less than their best). This also means setting aspirational goals for themselves and expecting to achieve them.

Secondly, learners should embrace challenges and enjoy hard work because they know it will help them to learn. This means actively engaging in lessons and readily accepting any new challenges that are presented. It also means exerting a lot of effort and engaging in deliberate

Community and the curriculum **155**

practice. It means pushing themselves in lessons, practising something repeatedly, and regarding additional study opportunities, such as homework, as an important way of consolidating and deepening their learning rather than as an onerous chore.

Thirdly, learners should seek out and welcome feedback. They should value other people's opinions and advice and use it to help them improve their work. Feedback should be given and received with kindness in a manner that is helpful and not unduly critical, and yet it should be constructive and specific about what needs to be improved.

Fourthly, learners should be resilient. By being resilient – not giving up easily when things get hard – they will overcome obstacles. Moreover, they will be happy to make mistakes because they know they will learn from them. In practice, this means that learners ask good questions in order to further their learning, and learners always try to solve problems for themselves before asking others for help.

Finally, learners should be inspired by other people's success. They should seek out examples of great work, discover what makes it great, then use this knowledge to inform their own work. They should take collective responsibility for the work of the class and have a vested interest in everyone's success. This means that learners support each other and encourage each other to succeed. This means that learners work well in groups and are confident in expressing their views and sharing their ideas. This means that learners are good at giving each other feedback that is kind, specific, and helpful.

15 Community and collaboration

 ## 3 Pace

Once we have instilled in learners a sense of purpose so that they know what they're learning, why they're learning it, and how that learning will be used in the future, and once we have set the bar high and instilled high expectations of what learners can achieve – creating a classroom culture of high challenge and low threat where we teach to the top – then we want to make sure that lessons are instilled with a sense of urgency. We want there to be an appropriate pace for learning so that learners cannot become passive. We want learners to feel a sense of progress, to know that they are moving relentlessly forwards and doing something worthwhile.

Pace starts with culture. We want to create a learning environment that is disciplined and orderly. We want to create a learning environment in which learners know what's expected of them and feel safe. And we want to create a learning environment in which learners are familiar with the habits and routines in place so that they do not have to dedicate much working memory capacity to it but can instead focus on the learning at hand.

Earlier, I shared six features of an effective learning environment, namely:

1. Learners feel welcomed

2. Learners feel valued

3. Learners are enthusiastic about learning

4. Learners are engaged in their learning

5. Learners are eager to experiment

6. Learners feel rewarded for their hard work

Once we've created an effective learning environment and motivated learners, we need to make sure they think hard but efficiently about the curriculum content we need them to learn.

First, we need to give learners work to do that's challenging but achievable because if the work's too easy, learners will complete it through habit; if the work's too hard, learners will be unable to complete it. In both cases, learning will fail.

Working on problems that are too easy or too difficult is not enjoyable because there is no sense of progress, and thus, we become frustrated. Working on problems that are pitched in our struggle zone, however, is rewarding.

This is why giving learners work to do that is too easy for them and which they can therefore accomplish without thinking – in the misguided belief that it will give them a sense of success and thus motivate them – doesn't work. Instead, we are motivated by thinking hard and overcoming difficulty; we are motivated by overcoming challenges.

To achieve this, sometimes, we need to place artificial barriers in the way of learners' initial encoding of information so that the information is stored more effectively and can more easily be retrieved later. These artificial barriers, or roadblocks in our thinking, are what Robert Bjork called 'desirable difficulties', which "slow down the apparent learning, but under most circumstances help long term retention, and help transfer of knowledge, from what you learnt to new situations".[1]

One problem with giving learners hard work to do is that a lack of space in working memory is a functional bottleneck of human cognition. We, therefore, need to help learners cheat their working memories. One way to cheat the limited size of working memory is through factual knowledge – the more information you have stored in long-term memory and the more mental maps or schema you have connecting this information together, the easier it is to process new information. Another way to cheat working memory is through the use of mnemonics and other memory aids, as well as by using dual coding.

Another aspect of 'pace' is the effective use of teacher explanations and modelling.

The best explanations present new material in small chunks and provide scaffolds and support. Here, we model a new procedure by, among other strategies, thinking aloud, guiding learners' initial practice, and providing learners with cues. Then, we provide supportive feedback and systematic corrections, giving learners 'fix-up' strategies and expert models of the completed task. Finally, we provide opportunities for extensive independent practice, affording learners plenty of chances to practice new knowledge and skills.

The best explanations tend to include:

1. **Metaphors and analogies** contextualise information so that abstract ideas or hitherto alien concepts are made concrete, tangible, and real and so that they are related to learners' own lives and experiences.

2. **Dual coding** combines verbal instructions as well as any text-based explanations displayed on the board or in handouts with visuals such as diagrams, charts, graphics, and moving images.

3. **Reciprocity** involves learners explaining concepts back to the teacher as well as to each other. This works on the basis that only once you teach something have you truly learned it.

4. **Models** provide exemplars of both good and bad work, as well as exemplars from a range of different contexts – in order to show learners what a final product should look like and what makes such products work.

Once we've explained and modelled new information, we need learners to engage with that information to deepen their understanding of it and improve their chances of transferring the information between contexts. As such, we need to provide plentiful opportunities for learners to engage in speaking and listening activities, and one of the best ways to do this is to ask questions.

In many ways, the art of asking good questions is what teaching is all about. Indeed, Socrates argued that "questioning is the only defensible form of teaching".

Dialogic teaching strategies make use of the power of talk to stimulate and extend learners' thinking, as well as to advance their learning and understanding. Dialogic teaching enables the teacher to diagnose and assess learners' understandings and misunderstandings through speaking, listening, and questioning.

4 Progress

Earlier, I argued that we should share our planning with learners so that they know what they're learning, why they're learning it, and how they'll apply that learning later. The same applies to assessment. We should share with learners how their progress will be assessed, when their progress will be assessed, and what we – and they – will do with the outcomes of these assessments. We need them to understand why assessment matters.

Before we can do that, however, *we* need to be confident that all our assessments are purposeful, that the process of assessment is efficient and effective, and that the resultant data will be valid and reliable.

When it comes to assessments being purposeful, as a handy rule of thumb, whenever we engage in any form of assessment, we should ask: Why? What is the point of this assessment? How will this assessment – and the data we collect from it – help learners to make better progress? If an assessment or data collection exercise is solely for management purposes rather than to help learners make progress, then in all good conscience, it should stop.

When it comes to efficiency, as well as considering the purpose of the assessment, we should think about the process by which we will assess, input data, and report the outcomes of the assessment. Here, it is useful to ask whether the process is as efficient as it can be or if it is unnecessarily burdensome. Consider also when and how often we are expected to assess and input data. Are we expected to engineer a test for learners, or can data be gathered in a more holistic, synoptic way? How is the data inputted? If it requires the use of technology, do we have easy access to it? What will be the outcome of this data collection exercise? What will be done with the data afterwards, and by whom?

And when it comes to the outcomes of assessments, we should consider how valid the data will be. By this, I don't mean how useful the data will be but rather how accurate and useable it will be. In other words, although we may have confidence that the data will be very useful in helping learners make better progress, the actual data we mine might not be as accurate as we hope, so all our subsequent actions may be futile or misguided.

To help answer this question of accuracy, we may wish to consider what is being assessed and if, indeed, that thing is assessable in a meaningful way. What, for example, are we comparing a learner's outcome to? Are those two things indeed comparable? Is the data we draw reliable?

Is it, for example, possible at this stage to assess progress, or might we be measuring a poor proxy for progress instead?

Next, we want to make sure that all our assessments of progress are meaningful, manageable, and motivating.

1. Meaningful

To my mind, marking and feedback have but one purpose: to help learners make better progress and achieve good outcomes. They might do this directly by providing cues to the learner about what to improve, and they might do it indirectly by providing assessment information to the teacher to guide their planning and teaching. Marking and feedback carried out for any other purpose are not, in my view, meaningful activities and – as well as being a waste of our precious time – can distract and indeed detract from this important goal.

Although a school's assessment policy may set broad guidelines about how often learners' work should be marked to ensure no learner falls through the net, it also needs to build in sufficient flexibility so that we can decide *how* to do it.

The nature and volume of marking and feedback necessarily varies by age group, subject, and what works best for the individual learner and for the piece of work being assessed.

2. Manageable

Marking and feedback should be proportionate. Any expectation on the frequency of marking should consider the complexity of marking and the volume of marking required in any given subject, qualification type, and phase and key stage of education.

There is no doubt that feedback is valuable, but if we are spending more time marking and giving feedback than learners are spending on a piece of work, then our priorities are skewed.

We need to be selective in what we mark. Marking everything is time-consuming and counter-productive. Feedback becomes a single grain of sand on a beach, ignored by the learner because of its sheer ubiquity. Therefore, we should identify the best assessment opportunities in each topic or module – this might be a synoptic piece that demonstrates learners' knowledge and understanding across a range of areas, or it might be the exam questions that garner the most marks.

3. Motivating

Marking can help motivate learners to make better progress. Short verbal feedback is often more motivational than long written comments on learners' work.

Too much feedback is not only harmful to teacher workload, but it can also become a disincentive for learners because there is too much information on which to focus and respond. What's more, too much feedback can reduce a learner's long-term retention and harm resilience. To build retention and resilience, learners need to be taught to check their own work and make improvements *before* the teacher marks it and gives feedback. Feedback should also prompt further thinking and drafting, perhaps by posing questions on which the learner must ruminate and act, as opposed to ready-made suggestions and solutions.

Feedback can be more motivating if it requires learners to think. For example, we might use comment-only marking more often as this engages learners because it requires them to act. Rather than correcting a learner's spelling, punctuation, and grammar, for instance, we might place a letter in the margin for each error in that line. For the higher-performing learners, we might simply put a dot in the margin for each error.

We might also make use of whole-class feedback rather than give individual comments. Whole-class feedback identifies the most common errors and uses this as a teaching opportunity that engages all learners rather than allowing some to sit passively whilst others are getting feedback.

The fourth P – 'progress' – is also about preparing learners for future success, and this requires us to think deeply about the purpose of education.

The best teachers understand what their learners need to know and do to progress and be successful. One way to do this is to ask what learners will need to know and do in our subject in five- or ten-years' time. What do we want them to remember and be able to apply – fluently and in multiple contexts – in order to consider ourselves successful?

This process is not meant to be reductive; it's not – or at least not solely – about the *functionality* of our subject discipline. Knowledge is important for its own sake because knowledge begets knowledge, and we want to create cultured young people who know about the world and how it works.

Ten classroom habits

To help put all these concepts into practice, here are ten impactful routines that teachers can embed in their daily practice to help ensure their classrooms are inclusive places for all learners to learn and to help ensure their lessons talk to learners' lived experiences.

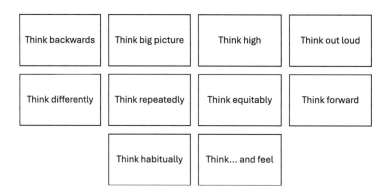

Figure 15.1 Ten classroom habits

1. Think backwards

The first classroom routine to embed is to think backwards. In other words, we need a laser-like clarity about the knowledge and skills we expect learners to have learned by the end of each lesson, and we should then plan backwards from there. If we, as teachers, can't articulate what we want learners to know and do at the end of each lesson, then it's unlikely that learners will know what's expected of them and that the lesson will lead to long-term learning.

When planning, we should therefore ask ourselves: What do I want learners to know and do at the end of this lesson that they didn't know and couldn't do at the beginning?

Then: What do I need learners to *think* about during this lesson in order for them to process and encode this knowledge and skills?

We might further consider how we will know if learners have acquired the knowledge and skills we set out for them to learn, how we will keep this knowledge and skills accessible to them over the long term, and how we will help learners to build upon this knowledge and skills in the future.

To sense-check our planning, we should routinely 'drop in' on learners and check that they all know:

● WHAT they are learning

● WHY they are learning it

● HOW that learning will be used and assessed later

2. Think about the big picture

The second classroom routine to embed is to think about the big picture so that we regard each lesson not in isolation but as one piece in a jigsaw. Put another way, there needs to be a logic to the order and organisation of lessons so that what we teach today builds upon and extends what we taught yesterday and is built upon and extended by what we teach tomorrow. Over time, there needs to be increasing challenges.

In practice, each lesson needs to provide opportunities for learners to activate their prior knowledge and then add to it, forging an ever more complex schema in learners' long-term memory.

Think of it like spinning plates: after we set a new plate off spinning, we need to circle back to all the previous plates we've spun and give them a quick turn to prevent them from losing momentum and crashing to the floor.

Sequencing in this way also allows us to articulate that bigger picture to learners, which, in turn, helps build learners' intrinsic motivation. It also ensures learners have the requisite knowledge to be able to understand new concepts – because we all process new abstract information within the context of what is already concrete and familiar.

In other words, articulating the bigger picture helps learners to cheat the limitations of their working memories and make better sense of the curriculum.

When planning, we should ask ourselves: What are the end points of my curriculum? This could be a scheme of work, a unit or topic, a year or key stage, or an entire phase of education. What matters is that we know what we want learners to know and do at the end of the sequence.

3. Think high

The third classroom routine to embed is to think high and teach to the top. This involves teaching the same ambitious, broad, and balanced curriculum to all learners and having high expectations of what all learners can learn – avoiding the temptation to 'dumb down' for some learners because of their starting points or additional and different needs.

Thinking high also involves teaching a curriculum that is sufficiently broad so as to prepare learners for what comes next but it must be taught with appropriate depth to ensure genuine understanding and aid transferability.

Furthermore, thinking high is about making sure all learners, not just the higher-performing ones, are stretched and challenged – both in terms of the pace and pitch of teaching and in the feedback given to help learners improve further.

I've already advocated one strategy which ensures all learners are stretched and challenged but prevents some learners from moving too far ahead of others: peer teaching. If the learners who have 'got it' teach those who have not, then the 'got its' are meaningfully engaged in retrieval practice and deepen their understanding of a concept by explaining it to someone else, while the 'have nots' are retaught a concept from a new angle.

We should ask ourselves: What does excellence look like? What standard of work should I expect from the highest-performing learners in my class? How can I model excellence and deconstruct it so that all learners can see how to produce work of a high standard?

Also: How can I maintain the integrity of my teaching sequence without holding some learners back or allowing others to flounder?

4. Think out loud

The fourth classroom routine to embed is to think out loud.

Firstly, we should start each new teaching sequence – whether that be a new concept, unit, or topic – with clear and insightful explanations. As I've already said, the best explanations are chunked into small steps, make use of analogies and metaphors to compare new, abstract information to what is already familiar and concrete to learners, and are dual-coded, combining verbal and visual information to aid learners' cognition.

Starting a new topic with teacher explanations – as opposed to discovery learning approaches – enables us to take ownership of the information flow and ensures learners do not waste too much time gathering information or develop unhelpful misunderstandings along the way.

Secondly, we should model excellence and, whilst doing so, make our invisible thought processes and decision-making visible to learners, thus ensuring our implicit expertise is explicit to the novice learner.

Thirdly, we should engage the class in co-construction, producing a model together. Here, learners provide the substance whilst we ask probing questions, drip-feed technical vocabulary, and pass the baton between learners so they can comment on and add to each other's contributions. We should also use questioning to engage learners and to provide ongoing formative feedback.

Fourthly, learners should produce a model independently – so as to engage in the cognitive process by themselves – and gather and act on feedback.

We should ask ourselves: What key information do I need learners to know upfront? What vocabulary do I need them to possess? How can I share this in an accessible way without overloading learners' working memories?

Then: How can I model excellence live in front of learners? What steps will I demonstrate, and how will I narrate my progress? How can I model metacognition and show learners how I deal with setbacks and improve my work as I go?

5. Think differently

The fifth classroom routine to embed is to think differently by planning a variety of learning activities for learners to engage in over time – with teacher explanations and modelling 'chunked' with questioning, practice activities, or group discussions which aid learners' retention and increase their attention spans.

Each lesson does not necessarily need to be varied, and I would never prescribe a set lesson structure. But, over a sequence of connected lessons, I do think there should be opportunities for learners to become increasingly independent and to engage in activities which allow them to become owners of their own and others' learning.

Pair work, group work, whole-class discussions, self- and peer-assessment, and suchlike are all great ways of ensuring learners are active participants in the process of learning, not just passive recipients of information. The trick is to gradually hand ownership of learning to learners by starting a new teaching sequence with the greatest level of control and slowly passing the reins to learners as they complete tasks for and by themselves.

6. Think repeatedly

The sixth classroom routine to embed is to think repeatedly by planning opportunities for learners to engage in some form of retrieval practice – and thus the building of schema – in every lesson. The shape and form of this retrieval practice – and when it happens within the lesson – is dependent on the context, so pragmatism is key, but retrieval practice needs to take place frequently to prevent knowledge decay and to help learners connect prior learning to new learning.

Thinking repeatedly is about engaging learners in activities that require them to activate prior learning and then add to it in order to spin ever-more complex webs of knowledge in long-term memory. These mental maps – or schema – help learners to think more efficiently and effectively.

Retrieval practice does not have to be convoluted, nor does it have to involve lots of planning. In fact, one particularly impactful form is *free recall,* whereby we greet learners at the door at the start of the lesson and give each of them a blank piece of paper. When they sit down, the task is to write down everything they can remember from the previous lesson. We might use this to unpack prior learning and to unmask any misconceptions, but we don't necessarily have to do anything. The simple act of learners retrieving from long-term memory what they've previously learned and writing it down is good enough!

7. Think equitably

The seventh classroom routine to embed is to think equitably by teaching all learners the same curriculum, thus ensuring equality, but making sure those learners with additional and different needs are supported to access that curriculum through adaptive teaching strategies, thus ensuring equity.

As I've already explained, thinking equitably is about giving those who start with less more help to access the same curriculum as their peers. The 'more' might take the form of task scaffolding whereby learners are given more detailed instructions, additional information such as a word bank, worked examples, or partially completed tasks (perhaps with stem sentences) in order to help them get started.

The key to success is that any additional scaffolding we put in place falls away as quickly as possible, ensuring learners become increasingly independent and can do the work for and by themselves. Otherwise, we are in danger of perpetuating learned helplessness.

8. Think forward

As well as knowing the bigger picture of learning, learners also need to know how, when, and why they will be assessed and how prior learning will be activated and built upon.

I've already suggested that learners should only be assessed when that assessment will lead to feedback and that feedback should only be given when there is time given in the lesson for them to process it, question it, and act upon it.

The results of assessments should then be used as learning opportunities – for example, in the form of whole class feedback on the most common errors – rather than simply drawing lines in the sand. In other words, feedback should be formative with actionable next steps.

The eighth classroom routine to embed, then, is to think forward – to ensure that learners are given feedback on which they can and do act in order to make progress.

In fact, the best feedback offers both feedback *and* feedforward: it tells learners where they are now, where they were, and, therefore, how far they've come and what they need to do to make further progress.

9. Think habitually

Practice makes permanent: the more learner habits we can establish, the lower the demand on their working memory will be, and thus, the more able they will be to rise to the challenge of hard work.

We should think: What do I want all learners to do every lesson? Whatever can be standardised and practised to the point of automaticity, should be!

As a starting point, as I suggested earlier, we might practise how learners enter our classroom, how we start lessons, how resources are handed out and returned, and how learners engage in whole class discussions (hands up or no hands up, active listening, commenting on what others say not how they say it or who they are, etc.), how learners self- and peer-assess and peer-teach, how learners respond to feedback, how learners try to overcome difficulties by using coping strategies and wall displays, etc., before seeking help from you, and so on.

As I explained earlier, we might also think about the social norms we want to establish in our classroom and the rewards and sanctions we apply when learners do or do not conform to those norms – working within the confines of your school's policies, of course.

Time spent practising daily routines at the start of the year or term will pay dividends later because we won't have to repeat instructions or tackle low-level disruption/non-compliance.

10. Think . . . and feel

The final classroom routine to embed is perhaps the hardest to teach but the most important: showing warmth towards learners and visibly caring about their success – something we'll quickly find is rewarded with their loyalty and hard work.

Warmth isn't about being fluffy and soft; it involves having high expectations of learners, both academically and in terms of their attitudes to learning, and explicitly teaching learners the study skills they need to access your curriculum, engage with it, and make progress.

Showing warmth is also about listening to and understanding learners, empathising with them, but not tolerating anything less than their best.

Note

1 Bjork, E., & Bjork, R. (2011). Making things hard on yourself, but in a good way: Creating desirable difficulties to enhance learning. In Gernsbacher et al. (Eds.), *Psychology and the real world: Essays illustrating fundamental contributions to society.* Worth Publishers.

Putting it all into practice

Targeting Tommy

Let's close the circle and return to the tale of Thomas and Tommy.

We know that Thomas is likely to win the race against Tommy at school and indeed at every juncture of their lives, not because he's brighter or harder working, but because he started halfway round the track and has more expensive running shoes.

But it doesn't have to be this way. Let's pull together all the advice contained in this book and draft a plan of action for our schools to help ensure Tommy's birth does not become his destiny . . .

Step 1: Take a learner-led approach

We now know that a label-led approach is misguided because it mistakes the label for an educational disadvantage, assumes all learners with the same label are the same, and isolates or – worse – stigmatises learners with labels. Not every learner who has a label will need special treatment, and just because a learner does not carry a label does not mean they will not be educationally disadvantaged in some way.

Taking a learner-led approach is about converting the *causes* of disadvantage into tangible classroom *consequences*. A cause might be living in a low-income home; a consequence of this might be gaps in vocabulary. The solution: explicit vocabulary instruction and the building of cultural capital.

Step 2: Focus on attendance

It all starts with attendance because if learners are not attending school, or at least not regularly and on time, then we cannot help them engage with their education, learn, and make progress, and we cannot identify additional needs and put in place the appropriate support. Attendance is also integral to building more equity in education because disadvantaged learners are more than twice as likely as their non-disadvantaged peers to be absent and persistently absent from school.

Putting it all into practice **167**

In practice, this means:

- Adopting two mantras:
  - Every day counts
  - Attendance is everyone's business
- Flipping the conversation:
  - Avoid the deficit model and headline statistics
  - Promote the benefits of good attendance
- Understanding the causes of absenteeism:
  - Anxiety and mental health issues
  - Poverty
  - Housing
  - Illness
  - Special educational needs and disabilities
- Taking a three-pronged approach:
  1. Address school factors: curriculum content; curriculum coverage; social and emotional environment; routines and expectations
  2. Address home factors: parental understanding and engagement; household routines and logistics; parental presence and support; socio-economic factors
  3. Address learner factors: academic barriers; social and emotional barriers; SEND and mental health; illness
- Following a 5P framework:
  1. Policy: inform parents of their legal obligations; share tangible benefits of good attendance beyond the academic; help parents make informed decisions; consult on and communicate the policy regularly and in accessible forms.
  2. Personalisation: *assess* the causes of absence; *plan* strategies with parents; *do* make reasonable adjustments and remove barriers to attendance; *review* the impact of interventions to develop institutional intelligence.
  3. Practice: exhibit high expectations by talking of lost learning; promote health and wellbeing benefits of good attendance; provide a planned programme of staff development; adopt evidence-informed approach to interventions; focus on celebrations over sanctions.
  4. Performance data: monitor 'live' attendance and take a no-tolerance approach to unexplained absences; analyse data to identify patterns and trends; provide reports to key stakeholders; use data to evaluate impact.

5. Parents: work with parents as partners, involving them early and often; treat parents with dignity and respect; ask what you can do to support them; regularly reiterate the attendance policy but personalise the message; send positive messages; reach out to the community to contact hard-to-reach parents.

Step 3: Focus on behaviours

Once learners are attending, we need them to develop appropriate behaviours for learning. Note the plural 'behaviours' because this is two-fold: First, learners need to be helped to conduct themselves appropriately and to comply with our rules and expectations; second, learners need to be helped to develop positive attitudes to learning and a raft of behaviours for learning so that they can access an increasingly challenging curriculum, actively engage with their studies, and make good progress.

In practice, this means:

- Creating a whole-school culture which promotes good behaviour:

  - Agree on the social norms that you want to see reproduced throughout the school community.

  - Communicate routines to staff and learners until they become automatic by demonstrating them and ensuring every aspect of school reinforces them.

  - Continuously cultivate the culture through staff training, the use of consequences, data monitoring, staff and learner surveys, and maintaining standards.

- Promoting an ethos of positive behaviour by being clear about which behaviours are permitted and which are prohibited and by setting out the values, attitudes, and beliefs you wish to promote.

  - Consult on and communicate a behaviour policy which includes information on purpose, people, process, professional development, progression, pastoral care, protection, and permitted and prohibited actions, and which is accessible, aligned, and all-inclusive.

  - Adopt the principles of openness, consistency, and fairness.

  - Actively teach learners how to behave appropriately through a behaviour curriculum which defines expected behaviours in school and articulates what they look like.

  - Make reasonable adjustments to social norms for learners who have additional and different needs, including those with a protected characteristic under the Equality Act 2010.

  - Ensure all staff model the behaviours they expect to see from others and uphold the school's culture.

- Establishing a classroom environment built of routines, regularly repeated and reinforced:

  - Attend to the beginning and end of lessons and any task transitions within lessons.

  - Establish clear routines for handing out resources and for engaging in classroom talk.

Putting it all into practice **169**

- Make reasonable adjustments to the environment, ensuring the classroom is quiet and distraction-free, is fitted with good lighting, heating, and ventilation, is visually attractive and inspiring yet is clutter-free.

- Instil a growth mindset through frequent, formative feedback, high levels of challenge for all, the welcoming of mistakes, opportunities for retrieval practice, and rewards for hard work and effort.

- Ensuring staff are appropriately skilled to manage learner behaviour in their classrooms:

  - Staff need to be able to promote interactions and relationships with all learners that are based on mutual respect, care, empathy, and warmth; they need to avoid negative emotions in interactions with learners; they need to be sensitive to the individual needs, emotions, culture, and beliefs of learners.

  - Staff need to promote a positive climate of learner-to-learner relationships, characterised by respect, trust, cooperation, and care, and motivate learners through feelings of competence, autonomy, and relatedness; staff need to create a climate of high expectations, with high challenge and high trust, so learners feel willing to have a go.

- Teaching metacognition by modelling the thinking processes of a self-regulated person.

  - Employ effective behaviour management strategies, including leading by example, staying positive, treating each day as a clean slate, ensuring all adults work together, rewarding the right behaviours, diverting low-level disruption, and using sanctions when appropriate.

  - Make reasonable adjustments to behaviour management strategies for those learners with additional needs and who face challenges when conforming to our expectations without reducing expectations or accepting inappropriate behaviour from some learners. The key is belonging. To achieve this, try to understand why some behaviours are more likely to be associated with particular types of SEND and mitigate these with, for example, short, planned movement breaks and adjusted seating plans.

- Establishing an effective system of consequences which is not only important to maintaining order in school but also teaches learners crucial life lessons:

  - Agree on a set of rules, rewards, and sanctions which provide clear boundaries that help make learners feel safe, add to the predictability of the classroom, and help prevent disruption.

  - Reward the right behaviours and give oxygen to those who deserve it most.

  - Be unafraid to use sanctions when appropriate, but make sure the learner is afforded the time and opportunity to rectify their mistakes and make choices about their future behaviour.

- Planning an effective programme of personal development which prepares all learners in school for their next steps:

  - Develop learners' self-efficacy by finding the bright spots, avoiding learned helplessness, giving learners ownership, and giving learners responsibility.

- Teach learners an effective programme of PSHE which helps learners to develop self-esteem and resilience, and communication skills such as advocacy, negotiation, and persuasion.

- Teach learners how to tell the story of their lives to improve their self-perception and help them develop a habit of questioning their own perceptions, beliefs, and ways of thinking.

- Teach learners how to manage their emotions, how to become aware of their strengths and weaknesses, how to be reflective, and how to learn from their experiences.

- Teach learners how to stay motivated by developing autonomy, self-efficacy, and mastery and by providing learners with a rationale for learning by sharing the 'big picture' with them.

Step 4: Focus on community

Once learners are attending and behaving appropriately and positively, we must focus on building a community around our learners by putting family first. Schools do not exist in isolation; they are a part of the community they serve.

Community is also about engaging with parents and families as partners in the process of educating their child, involving not just informing them on matters pertaining to their child's progress and wellbeing. Communication should be a dialogue, not a monologue, and be marked by dignity and respect. Our conversations should not apportion blame but ask how we can support parents to support their children.

In practice, this means:

- Making sure parental engagement is early, continuous, two-way, timely, relevant, useful, and multi-form.

- Making sure parental communications are clear, timely, acted upon, and consistent.

- Reaching the harder-to-reach parents of disadvantaged learners by being clear, respectful, empathetic, patient, open, and flexible.

- Fostering a sense of belonging and prizing the social and emotional development of learners as much as the academic.

- Talking to learners' lived experiences by assessing starting points and filling gaps in prior knowledge, ensuring the curriculum reflects learners' lives, and ensuring the curriculum takes learners beyond their own experiences.

- Establishing a programme of extra-curricular activities which provides all learners with equal access to opportunities to meet new people, explore new places, and do new things.

- Ensuring teaching has a purpose and is ambitious, progressive, and preparatory.

- Ensuring learning is pitched in learners' struggle zones by teaching to the top so that information is stored in and can be retrieved from long-term memory.

- Ensuring there is an appropriate pace to learning and that assessments are meaningful, manageable, and motivating so that they help learners make progress.

Let's put these actions into a plan . . .

Putting it all into practice **171**

Objectives	Current strengths	Areas for improvement	Actions required with timescales	Success criteria
Attendance				
1. To convince parents that every day counts				
2. To ensure that attendance is everyone's business				
3. To avoid the deficit model and headline statistics				
4. To promote the benefits of good attendance				
5. To better understand the causes of absence				
6. To address in-school factors (the push and pull of school)				
7. To address at-home factors				
8. To address learner-based factors				
9. To consult on and communicate an effective attendance policy				
10. To plan personalised attendance improvement strategies and make reasonable adjustments				
11. To exhibit high expectations and adopt an evidence-informed approach				
12. To monitor data live and analyse it for trends				
13. To work with parents as partners and personalise the messages				
Behaviours				
14. To agree on a set of social norms and embed them for all				
15. To communicate routines and ensure all staff model them				
16. To monitor behaviour data, including the impact of consequences				
17. To consult on and communicate an effective behaviour policy				
18. To adopt the principles of openness, consistency, and fairness				
19. To plan a behaviour curriculum to teach learners how to behave appropriately				

Figure 16.1 (Continued)

Objectives	Current strengths	Areas for improvement	Actions required with timescales	Success criteria
20. To make reasonable adjustments to behaviour expectations and social norms				
21. To establish routines for the beginnings and ends of lessons, task transitions, and regular activities				
22. To make reasonable adjustments to the learning environment, including the physical aspects				
23. To instil a growth mindset, which focusses on effort and hard work				
24. To ensure all staff treat all learners with dignity and respect and show empathy and warmth				
25. To ensure all staff have high expectations of all learners				
26. To embed consistent, positive behaviour management strategies in every classroom				
27. To agree on a set of rules, rewards, and sanctions and provide clear boundaries				
28. To focus on the positive reinforcement of good behaviours over the sanctioning of poor behaviours				
29. To explicitly teach learners how to develop self-efficacy and improve self-perception				
30. To plan an effective programme of PSHE focused on improving self-esteem, resilience, and communication				
31. To explicitly teach learners strategies for managing emotions and being self-aware and motivated				
Community				
32. To ensure parental engagement is early and continuous, to-way and timely				
33. To ensure all parental communications are clear, timely, acted upon, and consistent				
34. To treat hard-to-reach parents with respect and use community links as conduits of information				

Figure 16.1 (Continued)

Objectives	Current strengths	Areas for improvement	Actions required with timescales	Success criteria
35. To foster a sense of belonging focused on learners' social and emotional development				
36. To ensure the curriculum talks to learners' lived experiences and takes learners beyond those experiences to develop their empathy and tolerance				
37. To plan an effective programme of extra-curricular activities to which all learners have equitable access				
38. To ensure teaching has purpose and is ambitious, progressive, and preparatory				
39. To ensure learning is pitched in learners' struggle zones by teaching to the top so that information is stored in and can be retrieved from long-term memory				
40. To ensure there is an appropriate pace to learning and that assessments are meaningful, manageable, and motivating so that they help learners make progress				

Figure 16.1 Action plan

Index

autonomy, self-efficacy, and mastery 118

The Beautiful Risk of Education 101
behaviour curriculum 74–75
belonging 135
Better Health Every Mind Matters 56
Biesta, G. 101
Bosanquet, P. 106
Bounce 86
Bourdeiu, P. 136
Bristol City Council 62
Bronfenbrenner, U. 135

Children and Families Act 2014 95
Children's Commissioner 25, 37
The Chimp Paradox 116
classroom environment 76
classroom management 91
cognitive function 15
consequences 96
continuing professional development (CPD) 152
Covid 21
cultural capital 4, 16, 136
curriculum 144

Dickens, C. 101
dual professionalism 152
Dweck, C. 85, 86

Education Endowment Foundation (EEF) 51, 106
Education Support 56
education, health, and care plans (EHCPs) 49, 95

emotional intelligence 116
Equality Act 2010 44, 53, 94
extra curricular activities 16
extrinsic motivation 117

free school meals (FSM) 13

Gladwell, M. 86
Goleman, D. 116
Goudvis, A 140
Great Teaching Toolkit 88
The Guardian 23

Hard Times 101
Harvey, S. 140
Hattie, J. 130
housing 24
Hymen, P. 102

illness 25
intrinsic motivation 117

Jacobson, L. 85
Joseph Rowntree Foundation 15

Kahneman, D. 116
Keene, E. 139

The Matthew Effect 17
Mencap 78
mental health 16, 23, 54
mesosystem 135

metacognition 90, 120
Mindset 85

National Health Service (NHS) 37, 62
National Literacy Trust 139

oracy 103
Outliers 86

parental engagement 127
personal, social, health, and economic education
   (PSHE) 55, 110
Peters, S. (Professor) 116
poverty premium 15
Public First 21, 53
Pupil Premium 13

Radford, R. 106
reasonable adjustments 78, 94
Rosenthal, R. 85

Schema Theory 139
school culture 68
School-Home Support 24
self efficacy 104
self-regulation 120
SEND Code of Practice 2015 78, 79

social capital 136
Social Mobility Commission 141
special educational needs and disabilities (SEND)
   25–26
The Stories We Tell 112
Syed, M. 86

Taylor, C. 89
Teachers Standards 78
The 4Ps 144
The 5Ps for attendance 34
Thinking, Fast and Slow 116
Trades Union Congress 24

UN Convention on the Rights of the Child
   44
University of London Institute of Education 78
University of Salford 82

Visible Learning 130

Weale, M. 23
Webster, R. 106
Wiliam, D. 102
The Working Classroom 141

Zimmerman, S. 139

Printed in the United States
by Baker & Taylor Publisher Services